THE GREAT INVITATION

Books by
EMIL BRUNNER
published by The Westminster Press

The Great Invitation
Eternal Hope
The Misunderstanding of the Church
The Christian Doctrine of Creation and
Redemption, Dogmatics, Vol. II
The Scandal of Christianity
The Christian Doctrine of God, Dogmatics, Vol. I
Man in Revolt
The Mediator
The Divine Imperative
Revelation and Reason
The Divine-Human Encounter

THE
GREAT INVITATION
And Other Sermons

by

EMIL BRUNNER

translated by
HAROLD KNIGHT

PHILADELPHIA
THE WESTMINSTER PRESS

Published simultaneously in Great Britain
and the United States of America by The
Lutterworth Press of London and The
Westminster Press of Philadelphia

First Published in English in 1955

This book originally appeared as "Fraumünster-Predigten,"
Zwingli-Verlag, Zürich, 1953

Library of Congress Catalog Card No.: 55-8594

PRINTED IN THE UNITED STATES OF AMERICA

PREFACE

SINCE it became known that, accepting the invitation of the International Christian University of Tokyo, I would be going to live in Japan for some years, our cathedral congregation has expressed a wish that I would have published a number of sermons by way of compensation for oral preaching in the pulpit.

Printed sermons have always and increasingly seemed to me inadequate. For preaching is essentially a living occurrence which can only very imperfectly be crystallized in writing. For that reason I have up to the present carefully avoided the publication of sermons. But perhaps in this instance the special circumstances will justify a departure from the rule. It is a question here of sermons which without exception were preached in the Fraumünster in recent years.

Since my own time was fully taken up by the completion of a theological work and preparations for my new post, my son, H. H. Brunner, Dr. Theol., Pastor of Marthalen, offered to relieve me of the editorial work involved, and produced from my various notes and shorthand manuscripts both a printable and authentic text. I cordially thank him for this unselfish labour.

I dedicate this volume of sermons to the Fraumünster on the occasion of the jubilee celebrating its eleven hundred years of history. To look back on such a long period of church life makes one realize, with peculiar vividness, that each of us preachers is only one of many hundred links in the chain which binds our present-day worship of God with that of the apostolic communities. May this venerable and beautiful house of God for long be a place where the Word of God is faithfully preached and a believing congregation unites to praise God to its own spiritual fortification and comfort.

Zürich, August 1953.   EMIL BRUNNER

CONTENTS

CONTENTS

LORD, IS IT I?

Now when even was come, He was sitting at meat with the twelve disciples; and as they were eating, He said, Verily, I say unto you, that one of you shall betray me. And they were exceeding sorrowful, and began to say unto Him every one, Is it I, Lord? And He answered and said, He that dipped his hand with me in the dish, the same shall betray me. The Son of Man goeth, even as it is written of Him: but woe unto that man through whom the Son of Man is betrayed! good were it for that man if he had not been born. And Judas, which betrayed Him, answered and said, Is it I, Rabbi? He saith unto him, Thou hast said.

Matt. 26: 20–25

WE can make no better use of Passiontide than to conjure up afresh to ourselves the drama of the suffering and the dying of our Lord, and to accompany Him as it were on the way to the cross, bearing in mind that most challenging question of the disciples which stands in our text to-day: *"Lord, is it I?"* For the passion and death of our Lord is for us not merely one series of events alongside a multitude of others, but rather the central point in the whole Bible, the basic theme in that whole composition which is the history of humanity. For there happened there what happened nowhere else, what happened only there and then, once for all: the redemption of the world, which indeed took place for all, but which benefits only him who can ask the question, "Lord, is it I?" and to whom in consequence the conviction strikes home: Yes, you, precisely you, are responsible. All that was done on my behalf, I am he in whose stead Jesus suffers the punishment of the cross; it is I for whom the passion is borne: yes, it is indeed I.

First, our story stands so to speak under the shadow which the cross casts before it—that cross upon which Jesus will hang half a day later. The presentiment of what is to come hangs in the air in that small upper room where the disciples sit at table with their Master and eat the Last Supper. But even for Jesus Himself it is not yet quite simply predetermined that events must so shape themselves. That hour in the garden of Gethsemane has not yet come in which Jesus, troubled unto death, prays the Father that He would allow the cup of suffering to pass away from Him. On the other hand He has already predicted to the disciples many days previously that the Son of Man would be betrayed and crucified. And again during this meal Jesus will speak to His disciples those words in which He will explain to them and to us the meaning of His death as the effective operation and token of divine atonement. At this point we are faced by the impenetrable mystery of the divine humanity of Jesus who knows on the one hand what the divine will is and is wholly at one with it, and who yet on the other hand does not see it simply as something predetermined, but rather as something which is still in the balance, and therefore can still ask the Father to let the cup pass from Him. The narrative which we have just read gives us an insight into just this duality and tension.

The Lord has seated Himself at table with His twelve disciples. All twelve are there for the last time; on the way to Gethsemane, indeed as the solemn meal is partaken of, there are only eleven; for the twelfth has now gone his own way, that fearful way which must have a fearful end. Until this hour it had been impossible for the disciples to think otherwise than that they, the twelve, inseparably belonged to Jesus. It could never have entered their heads that one of them might not be present when the others were enjoying fellowship with Jesus. For not in vain had Jesus chosen twelve; He wished thus to make it clear that He was conscious of His membership in the people of Israel, composed as it was of twelve tribes, and that in all that He says, does and suffers He is primarily working on behalf of this His own people, the people of the Jews. Jesus Himself is of course by blood a Jew—born of the seed of David according to the flesh.

For all time it is to be made clear that Jesus does not disown

His Jewish blood and that He who inaugurates the new covenant desires that this His new covenant shall not be understood
as superseding the old covenant but as fulfilling it. So much the
number twelve is intended to signify—and the disciples correctly understood it in this sense when a few weeks later they fill
the gap left by the betrayal and suicide of Judas, electing in his
place another and a faithful disciple.

Still less for the disciples than for Jesus is the shape of things
to come, something clear, predetermined and foreknown. No
doubt Jesus spoke to them repeatedly of His imminent passion
and death. But they did not rightly appreciate His statements
and refused to believe them until at last compelled to do so.
That last and single stroke of the sword which one of the disciples executes as Jesus is taken prisoner in the garden of Gethsemane is a sufficient indication of this; only when Jesus is led
away captive and they themselves have taken flight did the
terrible truth dawn on them that Jesus was now about to die.
It may be indeed that Peter followed Him because he still
cherished a faint hope that all might in the end yet be well and
there be no sentence of death.

For this reason the word with which Jesus breaks silence
comes as a thunderclap: One of you will betray me. How could
such a thing be possible? And we, too, as we think of the treachery
of Judas, ask ourselves how it could be possible. The name of
Judas has become for us one of the most terrible names in the
whole history of humanity which nevertheless records many
terrible names—names which are especially terrible because of
the unfathomable mystery of evil. How was it possible, how can
such things be?

Closely linked with the inner sinister secret of the treachery
of Judas is the problem which the event presents in its external
aspect. We do not even know precisely in what the betrayal
consists. Was it only that he betrayed to the enemies of Jesus the
spot in which the Lord was accustomed to tarry at night, so that
they could conveniently arrest Him without any popular rising
—any resistance on the part of the masses who were friendly to
Jesus? Or did the betrayal consist in something quite different, in
the betrayal of the secret Messiahship, as many learned Biblical

critics suppose? And, furthermore, the motive of Judas is not clear. The evangelists suggest principally the motive of *avarice*. But could that really have been the deciding factor? Of course in recent years we have had to witness the sorry spectacle of men being prepared to betray their country for a few sordid pounds. But could Jesus really have chosen as one of His disciples a man who found it possible to betray his Master for such petty reasons? At this point we should perhaps incline to the view of those exegetes who put us on quite a different track by drawing our attention to the motive of disillusionment. Judas was disappointed by Jesus because disillusioned about the character of His Messiahship. He had obeyed the call of the Messiah because he had hoped that He would bring about the emancipation of Israel from the Roman oppressor and thus establish definitely a glorious and powerful Davidic kingdom.

But then he was compelled to recognize increasingly that Jesus was not that sort of Messiah. The story of the anointing at Bethany, when Jesus spoke plainly of His death as imminent, indicates a first step which Judas took to betray Jesus. On that occasion the eyes of Judas were opened; he must then have thought that he had been following a false Messiah and had been cheated. For Jesus had promised the coming of the kingdom of God and yet was now moving towards a criminal's death. He then decides that he no longer belongs to the circle of chosen disciples; on the contrary he proposes to have his revenge on the deceiver, the false Messiah. Hence he comes to his decision to betray Him.

I do not know whether such were really the actuating motives of Judas; no one can make categorical affirmations or denials in this matter. In the last resort we are compelled to confess: we do not know. That in itself is a puzzle but behind that puzzle lies a far deeper, more sinister, mystery: whatever were the thoughts and the motives of Judas, one thing is clear: he betrayed his Master, parted company with Him, and thus from being His disciple became quite unequivocally His enemy. That is the incomprehensible, awful, and sinister fact. A man who during the whole period of the Lord's public ministry companied with Him, hearing every one of His words, witnessing every one of His deeds, eating and drinking daily with Him and belonging to His most intimate circle of friends, to those who knew Him far better than any one else and to whom He confided everything, confided such things as He could not have confided to the crowd and who had thus been elected along with the other eleven to be the witness and apostle of the Gospel message—it was such an elect servant who was able to become the enemy of Jesus. Therein lies the essence of this dreadful and sinister mystery.

My friends, pause a moment to reflect upon this fact: it was actually possible for one of the disciples to become the enemy of Jesus and to betray Him to a hostile gang. That fact struck the disciples too as a gruesome and unfathomable mystery. Hence the evangelists Luke and John inserted into their narrative the gloss: "Then Satan entered into the heart of Judas called Iscariot." Here we are faced by an intractable secret, not the secret of God but that of Satan. I realize that there are many of us who do not believe in a devil and we are not required to believe in a devil, we are required to believe in God alone. But to those who assume that there is no devil I would like to say: you have not yet understood the depths of evil: you have not yet come to grips with this fact—Judas betrays his Lord. Nor have you yet measured the depths of your own wickedness.

But in the first shock of surprise when Jesus announced the imminence of His betrayal without naming the betrayer, the immediate reaction of the disciples was different. They did not primarily shudder to think that such a deed should be possible, they shuddered about themselves. They were seized by the awful fear: might I myself in the last resort be responsible for this treachery? "Lord, is it I?" My friends, I would like this "Lord, is it I?" now and ever anew to pierce us to our heart's core. Is it possible that I too might be capable of betraying Jesus and becoming His enemy?

Shortly afterwards, when Judas had stolen away, Jesus, looking into the face of the eleven, said something similar though not quite the same, and more in sadness than criticism: "Ye shall all be offended in me", i.e. be repelled and lose faith in me. And at the same moment He said to Peter in particular, to

Peter to whom only a short while previously He had declared that upon him He would build His church, "before the cock crow thou shalt deny me thrice". Denial, confusion and deviation is not as bad as treachery, as decisive hostility. Yet, if I may so say, the former tends in the same direction. And this being offended, dismayed and confused, Jesus predicted to all His disciples equally.

For this reason the question "Lord is it I?" is one which we must all put to ourselves. Am I not one who has already turned his back on Jesus and gone over to the enemy? Have I not already become offended and fallen into devious ways? Have I not already denied Him? When we seriously ask ourselves these questions and honestly examine our consciences, we must answer them in the affirmative. Theoretically, of course, in a simple credal catechism, we would repudiate such suggestions. No, I am not an enemy of Jesus; I believe in Him, I worship Him, I pray to Him, I confess Him to be the true Son of God and Saviour. That is all very well in so far as it goes. Many a one hits the bull's-eye in shooting practice, but on the field of battle, when surrounded by perils, he collapses and hits nothing. As long as we confine ourselves to a simple examination of our faith, in the abstract, apart from the test of events, we can confidently declare our faith in and love to Jesus, just as Peter was fully convinced that He would never deny His Lord. His indignant repudiation of the prediction of Jesus was, to be sure, spoken in all honesty—and yet he did deny Him three times before the night was over, before the cock crew. When perils press upon us and our life is endangered, then it is no longer so easy to confess Jesus. Then the question is just this: what do you now prefer to do, remain loyal to Jesus and die or deny Jesus and live?

I do not suggest that there is no value in confessing Jesus even when there is no danger in doing so. On the contrary, if we do not do that then, still less shall we be able to do it in the hour of crisis. But what our story teaches us is this: a confession which takes place on the shooting ground, and not in the field of battle, is not the decisive thing. In itself it offers no guarantee that we shall acquit ourselves in the moment of danger. We must indeed practise shooting, but only in the hour of battle is it seen how much has been gained thereby.

With the disciples we must be told that ever and again we abandon Jesus, turn our backs on Him, and so to speak for the moment surrender Him in favour of something which seems to us more important; thus in spite of everything we do what is not so very unlike the treachery of Judas, simply because we love ourselves and the world more dearly than we love our Lord, because time is always more precious to us than eternity. The sin which we commit consists in this; that we forget Jesus or as it were say to Him: Please leave me alone just now, I will come back to You again, but for the moment You are in my way. All sin consists in this kind of deviation from Jesus, this separation from Him, this pursuit of one's own paths, this denial and then, also, in the last resort, betrayal, the going over to the enemy.

And yet Jesus makes a big distinction between what Judas does and what the disciples will do on that fatal night. Only to Judas does He address the fearful saying: "It would have been better for that man not to have been born."

He does not say this even to Peter when He declares to him that he will deny Him thrice. We are rather too readily inclined to assert that all sins are equally important and that there is no reason to discriminate between them. Jesus makes a big distinction between the sin of Judas and that of Peter and of the other disciples. The distinction is this: neither Peter in his fear for his life, there in the court of the high priest's palace, nor the disciples who forsook Him and fled, intended finally to dissociate themselves from Jesus. Peter on hearing the cock crow went out and wept bitterly. Not so Judas. He took the irrevocable step of joining the enemies of Jesus. And when he eventually realized the nature of his deed in all clarity and insight he had no longer the power or courage or capacity to weep bitterly, to turn again and do penance. In that moment of realization he went out and hanged himself. There is a degree of dissociation from Jesus which can never be made good. Let us not think: *I* will never act as Judas did. You can never know in advance how far your unfaithfulness to Jesus will carry you. Let us rather constantly reflect that every sin has essentially something of the character of Judas' treachery about it, for every sin means to turn one's back on Jesus, to dissociate oneself from Him. Hence the more self-willed it is, the more deliberately we yield to temptation, so much the more does it resemble the deed of Judas, so much the more are we threatened by the danger of never again being able to return and find the tears of penitence.

But may our concluding reflection not be concerned with ourselves but with Jesus. For this drama turns upon Him, not upon us. Let us note one further point. Jesus wished to save Judas even at this eleventh hour, when the latter had already agreed with the enemies of Jesus to betray Him, even at the very moment when Judas was about to fulfil his intention. For this reason He says with fine reserve: One of you . . . He expresses Himself so because it is His last warning to Judas, a *Saviour's ultimatum* as it were. He still wants to keep faithful to Himself even that man who has already become a traitor—if it is at all possible. That reflection is a great consolation to us all. There is still room for repentance even though the possibility may be finally excluded. It is not yet too late as long as you can hear the voice of Jesus and allow it to strike home to your heart. "Whosoever cometh to me I will in no wise cast out."

The story of the treachery of Judas is followed immediately by that of the Last Supper: the New Covenant in my blood. No one is excluded from this covenant who seriously endeavours to find an entry. For Jesus Christ came into the world and died on the cross that all who believe in Him should not perish but have everlasting life. There are rooms in order to enter which you must stoop if you are not to knock your head. The cross of Jesus Christ is the door to communion with God and everlasting life. You must stoop if you wish to go in; otherwise you will knock your head and find no admittance. God grant that we may all rightly stoop under the door of the cross while as we gaze upon His cross we put to ourselves the question: "Lord, is it I?" and that we may receive the humbling and miraculously comforting answer: "*Yes, it is you.*"

THE TEMPORAL AND THE ETERNAL

Love never faileth: but whether there be prophecies, they shall be done away: whether there be tongues, they shall cease; whether there be knowledge, it shall be done away. For we know in part, and we prophesy in part: but when that which is perfect is come, that which is in part shall be done away. When I was a child, I spake as a child, I felt as a child, I thought as a child: now that I am become a man, I have put away childish things. For now we see in a mirror, darkly; but then face to face: now I know in part; but then I shall know even as also I have been known. But now abideth faith, hope, love, these three; and the greatest of these is love.

1 Cor. 13: 8–13

IN these latter years we have been made to experience in a particularly alarming manner how all things human are subject to the law of *change and decay*. Those of us who are older still remember how very different was the feeling of life in our younger days. We then considered so many things to be firmly and unshakably founded which have subsequently been dashed to pieces in the onward rush of the time stream. How fantastically has the map of Europe been changed, powerful empires have arisen and again vanished, the whole centre of gravity of the political world has completely shifted within the space of a few decades. The solid gains of civilization, such as the security of life and property and personal freedom which we held to be permanent attainments, have to a large extent disappeared, and, on the other hand, phenomena of earlier periods such as tyranny, barbarism, slavery, and the persecution of Christians which we had thought to have been permanently abolished, have again become a reality. The whole structure of life to its very centre seems convulsed, insecure and questioned.

Is there anything at all which has solidity? Is there anything for which the word of the poet is not valid when he says that everything which stands is only fit for destruction? Of course there is something exciting and fascinating about the idea that, as people say, things are in a state of flux. But life itself grows monstrous, indeed meaningless, if all is in a state of unending flux and imminent dissolution, just as what lends terror to an earthquake is precisely the fact that everything collapses, even the most solid thing—the earth itself. Of course we feel very comforted as we sing somewhat unreflectingly with Paul Gerhardt "All passes away . . ." but do we at the same time realize what it would mean if it were really true that all passes away? It would imply nothing less than that life as a whole is purposeless. And it is just that which is the feeling to which many to-day have succumbed and by which we are all more or less infected: everything is in a state of dissolution, nothing is unshakable, hence nothing abides; there is nothing which emerges permanently from the flux, there is no irremovable goal, no unchanging direction, no eternal meaning behind the revolutions of time. If that is indeed the case then life is truly a madhouse, full of sound and fury, signifying nothing.

The Word of Scripture which we have just read to some extent confirms this general impression. In this chapter too which is so often misunderstood and misapplied in a sentimental sense, the apostle Paul shows himself to be a great realist who sees things exactly as they are. Yes, he declares that transiency is truly the characteristic mark of our life here below. Even the greatest values which the Christian community has experienced and highly prizes he sees to be caught up in the unending flux of time. The word of the prophet, which in the main was the very life of primitive Christian worship, passes away—that for us so mysterious seizure by the divine spirit which he describes as speaking with tongues, also passes away; the recognition of ultimate divine truths to which the apostle Paul in particular had turned his mind and so largely contributed, again passes away. We might go on: not only all that we call culture and civilization, but also the Church itself, the sacraments and preaching—all that too passes away. For all this is integrally bound up with our earthly state, with temporality and imperfection—or, as we say to-day, with relativity. Even our apprehension of the divine revelation—this is what Paul means by knowledge—forms no exception. For, so reasons the apostle, what we now recognize as truth is something merely partial, not the rounded whole. Because and in so far as it is partial, it belongs to the sphere of the temporal and changing. It would have been good if the Church had taken more seriously this lesson of its greatest human teacher; it would then have been less easily a victim of the temptation to establish this or that formulation of its insight as an eternally valid, irrevocable dogma. For again and again it has been seen that even those supposed timelessly valid dogmas contained an element of the purely human and so of the changing. And it would be all to the good if precisely we theologians recalled more often this insight—that all our knowledge is partial. Then we would be less inclined to present our theses in an absolute and systematic manner and to accuse each other of heresy.

Please do not forget, Paul here suggests, that so long as you live on earth and are clothed in this earthly body, you go about, so to speak, in child's shoes. Maturity, true maturity of fulfilment, does not exist here. Even the greatest teachers err; there remains something unsatisfying and premature even in them and their thought. Even they must be corrected, even their message may not be taken without more ado as the last word of wisdom. This is felt above all by those who most zealously and passionately wrestle to attain truth. One of the most striking things about so doughty a Biblical exegete as Martin Luther— a feature which constantly reconciles us to much with which we are inclined to disagree in his writings—is that he emphasizes again and again that he is only a beginner and has not got beyond the rudiments of Scriptural interpretation, that every day he must learn afresh in a discipline which has no end. In fact it is precisely one of the notes of true greatness that a man should feel that he is only groping with the beginnings of insight and wisdom, always as it were only in the first stages, not only as regards knowledge but also in regard to the character of Christian living generally.

And our text suggests to us a second image on which to

ponder. All our knowledge is only a seeing through a glass darkly. As long as we see merely the reflection of a human being in a mirror, we do not make real contact with him; we do not see him face to face. And moreover what we thus see and recognize is in the last resort unsatisfying and incomplete. There clings to all that we can affirm about God, Jesus Christ, creation and redemption, a certain characteristic contradictoriness. Such doctrines are not lucid and self-evident like a theorem in Euclid, they are to be described rather as a mystery —a mystery which must always remain impenetrable to us. If we teach and speak as though we were dealing with self-evident mathematical truth we are teaching falsely; then the most essential thing is lacking, viz. the consciousness of mystery and impenetrability. Just for that reason our insights must be partial and always subject to correction. Unsolved and insoluble questions there must always be. We never reach the end; we are back always only at the beginning.

Is there then nothing which has unshakable solidity, of which we might say: That will abide, that is eternal? The apostle Paul is certainly a realist, but he is no relativist. He does not allow us to be engulfed in eddies of incertitude. We catch the reverberation of his words in another passage: "*For I am certain. . . .*" (Rom. 8: 38–39). In truth he preaches the gospel not as something uncertain, merely relative and transient. He knows of course that we carry this treasure in earthen vessels, that the treasure itself is embedded in human words and ideas and that the latter are temporal and passing because relative and incomplete. But the revelation is of God and therefore eternal. In what does this eternal and ultimately valid element consist? Do we somehow possess it otherwise than in the mode of merely human insights? Is there something in the actuality of Christian living of which we may and must say: there is the heart of the matter, the truly divine, which therefore abides unconditionally and absolutely?

To this our text gives answer, unlike many fine-spun theologies: yes, indeed, there is such an element, and it is *love*. But at this point we must beware lest we make a mistake which would confuse us about this very issue. Natural human love universally known is not here in question. The love of a mother, the love of husband and wife, the love of friends, the love of country—all are beautiful, good and necessary things, but they are not here in question. For all that is something natural, beautiful, of course, but still merely human. This Biblical message points to something which is not natural, but supernatural, something which is not human but wholly other, wholly divine.

What then has God disclosed to us in Jesus Christ? The fact that God is love. I wish I had the mastery of words that I might bring home to you the enormous significance of this affirmation which in our Sunday School days we sang about in a hymn I am tempted to describe as unfortunately sentimental: *"God is love."* It is the most amazing, incomprehensible pronouncement that was ever made in human language. Never previously had a philosopher or a treatise on religion formulated just this: God is love. If Plato or Aristotle had heard such a statement they would have shaken their heads and replied: "Man, you are mad, you do not know what you are talking about." How can God be love, indeed how can God experience love at all, since He has all and needs nothing and is wholly self-sufficient? What we are accustomed to call love is always a need for completion, a striving after something which one feels the lack of.

It is only within the sphere of Biblical revelation that love is described in exactly the opposite way. There we hear about a love which does not desire anything but simply bestows itself—a love which does not spring from any need or lack but has its source in overflowing richness and plenitude of life. "God loves you" does not imply "God needs you or longs for you" but that He gives and sacrifices Himself for your sake. Because of that the cross of Jesus Christ is the revelation of divine love, of the love which God not merely has but which is His very life. This love, true love, self-bestowing love, as opposed to claimful love, love which flows from inexhaustible wealth rather than from want—just that is the being of God. And if we propose to speak of God then we must speak of Him in terms of such love.

But I have not yet expressed the matter rightly. We only view it from the right angle when we bring into play the second person singular. God loves *you*. He wills to bestow Himself upon *you*. He wills to have fellowship with you, with you in whom He can find nothing lovely, simply because He wills to impart to you what is worthy of love—Himself. Consider well, this message comes to you not from some human source, from some religion or philosophy. It is addressed to you solely and exclusively in the glad tidings of Jesus Christ. God loves you, sinful man. God loves you and comes to seek you, as the shepherd seeks his lost sheep, the woman her lost coin, to find which she upsets the whole house. Yes, God has upset the whole universe in order to find you, His lost coin. He has come to us in the form of man, in the form of a crucified Saviour, so that no one can say: it is not me He is looking for, He does not want to know me. It is just you He seeks, you who feel so unworthy of being loved by Him. Just that is the meaning of the Gospel.

Thus God addresses you now in these words of mine and otherwise in the whole Bible. What answer will you make to Him? What answer would God like to have from you? What does He expect? He would like, He expects, that you quite simply believe what He says, that you accept it and rejoice because He loves you. That is what the New Testament means by faith. This utter simplicity of heart which causes you to accept the proffered love of God, to overcome your doubt that it might not be so, might not be God who is so speaking, and to take His outstretched hand.

And what happens now when you really do this, when with all your heart you grasp the love of God offered to you in Jesus Christ? Look, you do not then merely acquire the love of God, but it is rather that the love of God then penetrates your being with the result that a new life begins in you. Then you become a being who loves, then there grows in your garden something which is not of this world and its glory which passeth away, but a plant of divine heavenly and eternal origin—nothing other than this very love which flows from the heart of God Himself. This love, our text assures us, cannot pass away because it is eternal in its very essence. It is the thing with which all life is concerned and for the achievement of which we and the whole world have been created. It constitutes our eternal end, it is eternal life. It alone remains when all else passes away because it has its source wholly in the being of God, in eternity.

What then are we to say about the relationship of faith and love? Simply this: faith is the opening of the human heart to the penetration of divine love. It is the human hand which grips the proffered love of God. Faith is so important because it is the power by which we appropriate that love. And yet faith itself is not eternal but transient. For at the last it must so be that we need no longer believe because we shall live utterly in the animating presence of the love of God. But in the present order faith must always utter its "in spite of": in spite of the fact that I am a sinner God loves me. In spite of the fact that the world is so loveless, God the Creator and Lord of the world is love. In spite of the fact that Jesus Christ is the Crucified, He is the Son of God who took upon Him our flesh, who for our sakes became man, the incarnate love of God. In spite of the fact that I shall die, there is in me, inwoven into the roots of my being, the eternal love of God, the very life of eternity triumphant over death. This "in spite of" is nothing else but an expression of that obscurity which causes us to see only through a glass darkly. But there will come a time when the "in spite of" vanishes away. There will come a time when the opposition between sinful humanity and the divine is overcome and ceases to be. Then we shall no longer be confined to this earthly imperfect mode of the knowledge of God. Such knowledge will then be transcended by something far higher, namely, by the vision face to face. And therein lies the perfect and unchanging, towards which by faith our sure and certain hope is directed.

Faith knows that such is the eternal end. But so long as we must live by faith we have not yet attained it. Hence the end is always something other than what we now enjoy. We cherish the goal in the form of *hope*, a securely based, firm and steadfast hope, but nevertheless only hope. But when the end is reached and fulfilment comes, then we shall experience it no longer as hope but as plenitude of life and presence. For that reason, then, hope too, like faith, will vanish away. One thing will then remain unchanged: the love of God which we now apprehend in our hearts by faith. That does not pass away, nor does it need to be transformed. It is the unchanging and eternal, the being of God Himself, eternal life.

Now remain faith, hope and love, these three. Faith, the unsealing of the heart, the hand outstretched to make our own the love of God; hope which assures us of future fulfilment by the perfecting of our fellowship with God; and love. Faith looks back to what God has done and imparted. It sees how God cancels our past sins and forgives us in the name of Jesus Christ. Faith appropriates that past event in which God founds our life anew as the life of children of God who through the covenant of Jesus Christ have been adopted out of the status of aliens into that of sons of God.

By faith we live to-day in the power of what God has once done. And on the other hand hope points to the future of which we are already heirs, but which we do not inherit so long as we remain in this earthly fleshly life. By hope we hold fast to our future consummation as a good which really belongs to us through the work of Jesus Christ. As faith is concerned with the past and hope with the future, so love gives us fullness of life in the present. For the love of God is shed abroad in our hearts and we have appropriated the gift by faith. But this divine love is effectively present with us and makes us truly alive in the present. For where love is, there arises *plenitude of being and reality in the present moment*; where love is not, one is not truly alive to the urgencies of the present, but lives in regret and grief for the past, or in anxiety about the future. Solely through the power of love, can we be creatively alive in communion with our fellow men, really devoted to them and sensitive to their needs, so that they note of us: such a one is truly attentive to me, his heart is not elsewhere. But love is above all things the eternal "now"—that which fills eternity with its radiance and joy, and in the power of which God will be fully present to us and we to Him.

And thus of these three theological virtues, which are so closely interwoven, love is the greatest. Faith is not God Himself. God does not believe. And hope is not God, for God does not hope. But God is love, for God Himself loves and is love in its changeless living reality. Because God is greater than all things, therefore love is greater than any other virtue, greater even than faith and hope.

Let not your hearts be troubled about the transiency of all earthly things: only be steadfast through faith and hope in the love of God. That is the crucial issue. Whoever can thus stand fast, can do the best of which any human being is capable. And whoever cannot do that, falls short of the best, however able, however great a genius he may be in other respects. The changeless and abiding is love, is God. All else passes away: that alone remains. All else is only reflected light, reflected in the painted dome of earthly life. But love is the white radiance of eternity. Therefore let us live in the strength of love, which God has bestowed upon us in our Lord Jesus Christ.

THE ROCK ON WHICH THE CHURCH
IS BUILT

Reformation Sunday Sermon

Now when Jesus came into the parts of Caesarea Philippi, He asked His disciples, saying, Who do men say that the Son of Man is? And they said, Some say John the Baptist; some, Elijah; and others, Jeremiah, or one of the prophets. He saith unto them, But who say ye that I am? And Simon Peter answered and said, Thou art the Christ, the Son of the living God. And Jesus answered and said unto him, Blessed art thou, Simon Bar-Jonah: for flesh and blood hath not revealed it unto thee, but my Father which is in heaven. And I also say unto thee, that thou art Peter, and upon this rock I will build my church; and the gates of Hades shall not prevail against it. I will give unto thee the keys of the kingdom of heaven: and whatsoever thou shalt bind on earth shall be bound in heaven: and whatsoever thou shalt loose on earth shall be loosed in heaven.

Matt. 16: 13–19

*T*HOU *art Peter, and upon this rock I will build my church.* These momentous words are inscribed in colossal gold letters on the interior of the cupola of St. Peter's at Rome, and constitute as it were the foundation statute of the Roman Catholic Church. To-day we celebrate Reformation Sunday and invoke the memory of October 31, 1517. On that day Martin Luther nailed his 95 theses to the door of the cathedral church of Wittenberg and thus inaugurated the Reformation movement. In these theses, which are concerned with the true nature of penitence, he attacked a focal point of Roman Catholic teaching and practice and thus, although he did not know it at the time, challenged the Church to battle. The purpose of our celebration to-day is to consider afresh what the Reformation means to us and why we wish to be not Roman Catholic, but Reformed and Evangelical.

Is it not then that the Church of Rome is supported in its claims by Holy Scripture, by the word of the Lord Jesus Christ Himself, and does it not with justice appeal to that word which describes Peter as the foundation and the rock on which the Church is built?

This word addressed to Peter was spoken in a decisive and critical hour of the Master's life. The Lord, accompanied by His twelve disciples, had left the country in order to be alone with them for a while. Caesarea Philippi lay at that time in heathen territory. There He was alone with His most intimate circle of friends; there no adoring crowd followed Him, to hear His words or to be healed. There He had time to devote Himself to His closest friends whom He had chosen to be the messengers of the gospel in the future. And it was in such circumstances that for the first time He put to them the question: " *Who do you say that I am?* "

Why does Jesus ask such a question? Had He been an ordinary man we should feel a question like that to be curiously out of taste and suggestive of conceit. It is certainly not a sign of inner greatness for a man to ask what opinion is held about him. If Jesus does so, the question does not imply that He wishes to ascertain whether the world is paying Him all necessary tribute. But why does Jesus ask, instead of quite simply stating who He is? The fact that He asks, that He does not Himself declare His status, leads us straight into the heart of the gospel.

Jesus asks rather than gives authoritative instruction about Himself because He wishes the disciples freely to recognize the truth. This fact is of the greatest importance for us also. Many suppose that we should believe in Jesus as the Son of God because Holy Scripture declares Him to be such. One must quite simply believe it, they say, because it stands thus in the Bible. It is just that point of view which is false. We must not believe solely because the Bible so instructs us. We must *ourselves spontaneously recognize* this doctrine to be the truth which God is disclosing to us. We are not to believe on the authority of human teaching, not even on that of prophets and apostles. We are not to believe because the doctrine is enshrined in the Bible.

Our faith must not be of such a type that we believe first in the Bible and then in Jesus Christ. It is just that type of faith—authoritarian faith—which is Catholic rather than evangelical. The Catholic Christian must believe what the Church teaches. He submits himself primarily to the authority of the Church. He believes in Jesus because the Church bids him do so. That is a servile and spurious type of faith. True faith is of a different kind. True faith is essentially a matter of free recognition and insight. True faith in Jesus Christ arises precisely as the faith of the apostles arose. They had no scripture to tell them that Jesus was the Christ. But they had Jesus who was with them daily, whose deeds they saw, whose words they heard, whose bearing and attitudes they witnessed, whose voice sounded in their ears and whose look encountered theirs. As John says: "What we have heard, what our eyes have seen and our hands have handled —Jesus—declare we unto you" (1 John 1: 1). We must not believe on the authority of Peter or John or Paul that God comes to meet us in Jesus Christ. For in that case our faith would be faith in Peter, John or Paul. We are to know the truth in freedom. For that reason Jesus did not tell the disciples the truth but enquired of them whether they had at last come freely to recognize it for themselves.

Have you yourselves come to know the truth? When you read the gospels and study the accounts of the deeds, words, passion and death of Jesus, and consider further the testimony borne by the apostles in their epistles to their congregations, does all this affect you in such a way that the insight flashes upon you: in this man we are in the presence of God Himself? His words are God's words, His deeds are God's deeds, His being is the very being of God, His love the love of God Himself? And could you therefore attest as your own intimate personal faith that God was in Christ reconciling the world unto Himself? It is well with you if that is the case, for then you have your own living truly evangelical faith and no mere Catholic faith. Then you have encountered the living God Himself in the word of Jesus and the word about Jesus. Then in the word of the Bible you have heard the word of God and God Himself has spoken to you in His incarnate word, His Son Jesus Christ. Then your faith consists in a dynamic personal relationship with God and with Jesus Christ His Son.

Peter was the first man to recognize and confess Jesus as the Christ. To the question: "Who do you say that I am?" he answers: "Truly, Thou art the Christ (the Messiah), the Son of the living God." It is as if in the reply of Jesus to Peter's confession we can still detect a note of excitement: have you really won this insight, has God thus unsealed your eyes, have you—at last —got so far as to recognize that I am your Lord and Saviour? Hence Jesus answers with a tone of heartfelt joy and felicity: "Blessed art thou, Simon Bar-Jonah, for flesh and blood hath not revealed it unto thee, but my Father which is in heaven." Scarcely was Jesus accustomed to address Peter thus: Simon, son of Jonah. This especially solemn mode of address was meant to express the fact that here and now something of extraordinary importance had taken place in virtue of which also this name Peter or Simon would always be endowed with peculiar significance.

I should like to answer briefly two questions which constantly arise. Firstly, *how does one attain faith?* Faith is reached not simply by submitting to what the Church or the Bible teaches, but in proportion as a man through the preaching of the Church and the witness of Holy Scripture is instructed and moved by the voice of God Himself. And this comes about when one no longer as formerly defends oneself over against God, insisting upon one's own freedom and trusting in one's own intrinsic merits, but is ready to confess that one is an impotent sinner. We arrive at a true faith when we are ready to receive the forgiveness of our sins and to recognize God as the Lord of our lives. That is the right way to faith which the reformers again opened up after it had been for centuries—if not entirely yet almost entirely—concealed and blocked by the Roman Church.

The second question is: *Why must we believe in Jesus Christ at all? Does it not suffice to believe in God?* This question again springs from a false authoritarian mode of conceiving faith. The point is that we do not *have* to believe at all either in God or in Jesus Christ. It is of no avail to believe because we have

been told that we ought to believe. Belief is God's gift of grace
and faith is just this—that we are given eyes to see and ears to
hear. God Himself speaks with us. God gives Himself to us
that we might see and know Him and He does that precisely
through Jesus Christ. Whosoever sees me sees the Father. God
has made Himself visible to us in Jesus Christ. As in olden
times a knight lifted his visor in order to reveal his identity, so
God in Jesus Christ has disclosed His essential being that was
formerly hidden. God says: behold Him and you behold Me.
Hear Him and you hear Me. Serve Him and you are serving
Me; love Him and you are loving Me. He is a partaker of your
human nature and therefore you can understand Him. But He
is not merely a partaker of My divine nature, He is co-equal
with Me, and thus you can apprehend Me in Him. We do not
have to believe in God and we do not have to believe in Jesus
Christ, but we can come to God the Father through faith in
Jesus Christ the Son. For in Jesus we know God as Father and as
grace-giving Lord. Through Him we receive the atoning forgiveness of God. There are not two beings but One in whom
we must believe: God in Jesus Christ. That is evangelical faith.
Such faith has a twofold implication: it implies God's gift to us
in Jesus Christ who is also the Mediator of our knowledge of
God—a knowledge which means necessarily the confession of
our sin and the joyful acceptance in thankfulness of divine
grace. Whoever is not prepared to acknowledge himself to
be a sinner and to allow the grace of God to be bestowed
upon him, cannot attain faith. But whoever is ready to
undergo that discipline reaches the state of mind we call
faith.

The recognition that Jesus is Messiah, Redeemer, and Son of
God, comes to us as the gift of God Himself. Truly flesh and
blood hath not revealed it to thee. Neither priest, bishop nor
pope nor even the Bible, neither Paul nor Peter nor John can
give us this insight—only God Himself. The Father in heaven
hath revealed it to thee. As when a shutter is thrown back and
we look out into the open spaces beyond, so in Jesus Christ we
look without hindrance into the countenance of the gracious
God. And this unclouded vision is brought about by the action

of the Holy Spirit, if only we are ready to receive it and to accept as sinners the forgiveness of God.

But then what is the meaning of the expression about the Church? Does that phrase really imply the Roman Catholic Church as known to history? No justification for its claims is to be found in this text. Peter is the rock of the Church, i.e. of the communion of Jesus Christ scattered throughout the whole world, because He is the first to have recognized Jesus as the Christ and to have confessed His Lordship. For that reason a new name is given to him now only in this crucial hour. Previously he had been called simply Simon son of Jonas. From now on he is called Cephas or Petros, the man of rock. He is the rocklike basis on which the Church is built. He is so because the Christian community springs from *the insight which impelled him to confess* the Christ and from the consequent proclamation of Jesus as the Christ. All that we know of Jesus, all that we understand as the being and work of Jesus, hence the whole structure of our Christian faith and our standing as Christians, our whole Christian vision and communion, rests on this basis of apostolic testimony. Of course the apostles too are only men of flesh and blood. They too are such as need and have Christ as their Saviour. But in contrast to us they stand in a special relationship to Jesus because they are the first witnesses on whose life and testimony the faith and fellowship of all later disciples or Christians have been built up. We all stand on the rock of Peter, i.e. of the living Word of God which they are the first to have declared and preached. But Peter is primary because he first recognized and confessed Jesus as Lord. The apostolate is therefore a unique phenomenon. Only the apostles as the primal witnesses constitute the basis on which the Church is built and on which the preaching of subsequent witnesses can rest.

Hence it represents a reversal of what Jesus declared in His words to Peter, when the apostolic dignity of the latter is transmitted to later disciples who describe themselves as his successors. Even if Peter had been in Rome—which is very uncertain; even though Peter had been bishop of Rome—which is as good as excluded by the fact that an apostle was not a bishop and what was later meant by that term is altogether foreign to primitive Christianity—he would still not have been the man of rock in his capacity as bishop of Rome but in his capacity as apostle. It is just the apostolic dignity which is not transmissible, for it is by its nature unique. The apostles are the first witnesses to Jesus the Christ. Their dignity and special status consists in this fact of primacy and as such it is essentially not transmissible. The later bishops of Rome—who at a still later time were termed popes—are precisely not the primary witnesses, not apostles. The theory that Jesus wished to confer upon them as successors of Peter, in the see of Rome, the selfsame dignity is one which has no basis in fact and which contradicts the clear meaning of this description of Peter as the primary apostle. The affirmation *Thou art Peter*. . . is wrongly inscribed on the cupola of St. Peter's. A false meaning has been attached to this phrase, in sharp contradiction to its true meaning.

It is just this falsity which the Reformers perceived. They realized the lack of justification in the papal claim to authority and dominion and thus restored the true and original meaning of faith, the word of God and the Church. That was the essential work of the Reformation, to restore the original understanding of faith, the divine word, and the Church. Thus they freed us from a servitude to man which blocks the way to true faith. Of course this is only valid in so far as we Protestants have true faith and live by it. Unfortunately there are many Reformed Christians for whom the whole essence of their religion is limited to the fact that they are not Catholics. To such I must say that there are to-day and always have been Catholic Christians who are far better disciples of Jesus Christ than many Reformed Christians. And one is compelled to add that our Reformed Church has many defects, so that in certain respects one must admit that Catholics have the advantage over us. But one advantage we have over them and that is the chief point: we again and again realize how fallible, frail and imperfect this our Church is. As Reformed Christians we know that the Reformed Church is only true to its essential character when it is ever anew in the process of reformation. And thus we realize further that one is only a true Reformed Christian when one's heart is right in the sight of God. Hence, my friends, let our prayer be, and may each one of you offer this prayer in his heart in all sincerity and truth: *we long for the reformation of our Church and we long for and struggle to bring about our own reformation.* How urgently we need it! Or is it possible that you feel very differently about the matter? For myself, I must pray God every day that He will reform me. I am not yet reformed; God must still reform me. Every single member of the Church needs reformation, needs a new orientation of life, the new creation in Jesus Christ.

The gates of hell shall not prevail against it. The Christian fellowship is an eternal kingdom. Whosoever belongs to Jesus the Risen Lord is sealed for eternal life. And the promise of God in Jesus Christ is that always even unto the end of the world there will be a Christian community believing in Jesus as the Christ, and delivered by Him not only from sin but also from the fear of death or of the third world war and the atom bomb, because it realizes that all these things can only kill the body, not the soul.

The keys of the kingdom of heaven, however, which the Lord in His answer hands over to Peter do not symbolize any papistic powers of government but quite simply the gospel of reconciliation by which the kingdom of heaven is made accessible to the believer. Again, to bind and to loose means nothing other than the effect of the operation of God's word towards man. It condemns the impenitent but it frees the penitent through the message of reconciliation. It closes the doors of the kingdom against the proud and self-righteous, and opens them to the broken and contrite in spirit. Peter is endowed with this authority because he is the bearer of the Word of God. At Pentecost he exercised it for the first time. There the first stones were added to the foundation: three thousand souls at once. There for the first time the gates of heaven were opened and souls were released from their bondage, and judgment was declared to those who were not willing to repent. And thus his word, which is nothing other than the Word of God, exercises its effects up to the present day. May it open the kingdom of heaven to us all and lead us to life-giving penitence.

THE GREAT INVITATION

But He said unto him, A certain man made a great supper; and he bade many: and he sent forth his servant at supper time to say to them that were bidden, Come, for all things are now ready. And they all with one consent began to make excuse. The first said unto him, I have bought a field, and I must needs go out and see it: I pray thee have me excused. And another said, I have bought five yoke of oxen, and I go to prove them: I pray thee have me excused. And another said, I have married a wife, and therefore I cannot come. And the servant came, and told his lord these things. Then the master of the house being angry said to his servant, Go out quickly into the streets and lanes of the city, and bring in hither the poor and maimed and blind and lame. And the servant said, Lord, what thou didst command is done, and yet there is room. And the lord said unto the servant, Go out into the highways and hedges, and constrain them to come in, that my house may be filled. For I say unto you, that none of those men which were bidden shall taste of my supper.

Luke 14: 16–24

TO-DAY we often hear it said: one hardly dare think about the future. It is better not to allow one's thoughts to dwell upon what may or will happen. There are many Christians also who think and speak like this. But in the gospel and in the life of the first Christian community it was not so. There the future was precisely what people thought much about and anticipated with keen and joyful expectation. For there the future meant the coming of the Lord Jesus Christ, and to that event they looked forward, as it is said in I Peter, "*with unspeakable joy*". In our parable, too, which the Lord narrated at a meal taken in the house of the pious man who was His host, it is a question of the future. This parable of the great supper might also be entitled: *the great invitation*. The whole gospel is an invi-

34

tation. The prophets and after them Jesus the Son of God Himself came to issue an invitation to men. For what end or to what
precisely do they invite us? This parable gives us the answer: to
the great feast in the kingdom of God. This feast means table
fellowship with the Host, glorious and eternal communion with
the living God who is our Creator and the Lord of our future.

Thus it is a question of the great and splendid future—that
future which is the fundamental theme of the gospel and which
filled the hearts of the first Christians with joy unspeakable.
Why is it that we Christians to-day experience and manifest so
little of this unspeakable joy concerning the future, the kingdom of God which is coming upon us?—for that is the essential
meaning of the word future. When we are in a position to look
forward to something good we cannot but feel a certain eager
expectancy. We look forward even though the good which
we anticipate is long in coming and between our present situation and that future good all sorts of trials await us. Just think
how we look forward to Christmas in spite of the fact that
beforehand there is much heavy work that we must get
through. In our thought we leap over the weeks of painful toil
in order to fix our minds on what is to come, on the glad and
holy festival celebrated in chant and hymn. The future towards
which our thought is directed is not only something which will
materialize at a certain date but, properly speaking, it is what
gives tone and inspiration to our life here and now. A man who
sees no future for himself is melancholy and depressed, lacking
in courage and broken in spirit. A man who has reason to look
forward to the future is eager and courageous. He hastens forward to meet it as it were with joyful stride. He is animated by
the thought of it and the whole direction of his life is determined by it.

We men are so made that we must live in this forward-look-
ing way and that our life inevitably consists in an anticipation
of the future. It is for this reason that the question of the future
and of our hope in it is so important. What then are we to
think of our future? It is of course utterly unknown to us and
in so far as we are able to foresee it somewhat it hardly suggests
that we can look forward to it with eagerness. When we think

of the concrete possibilities which the immediate future holds, our minds fly at once to all that we read in the newspapers. We inevitably think of the possibility of a third world war or other gloomy political events which hang over us like threatening storm clouds. And when we think of our own personal ultimate destiny we cannot avoid the thought that the final thing we know about the future is just the fact that we must die. How in such circumstances could one look forward to the future with any eagerness of anticipation?

But we Christians to whom the gospel has been preached, and who are ready to believe it, must not confine ourselves to the picture of the future which we can conjure up in our own minds but must look beyond it to the vision of the future which the Lord Jesus Christ proclaims to us with the fullness of divine authority: the great supper, the eternal future, everlasting life in communion with God and all our brothers and sisters in His eternal kingdom.

To this great feast we are all invited; all of us without exception are invited to look forward to this consummation, this most perfect conceivable goal, and to appropriate it as our own. It does not come to us automatically; we are to accept the invitation; we must exert ourselves to lay hold of it. But the invitation is open to us all. And now in the parable of the Lord the unbelievable thing happens: the invitation is not accepted, all sorts of excuses are invented in apology and every imaginable loophole of escape is ingeniously devised. Men do not go to the feast. And that brings me back to the question which I put to you at the beginning: why do we fail to anticipate the future with joy? The answer can only be: because we do not truly accept the invitation offered to us. Because we do not truly believe in the reality of it, or because we think that there are more important things to think about.

I am not now speaking of unbelievers, of the heathen (I shall speak of them later), but of Christians. For this parable is concerned precisely with believers themselves, with the pious, who do not accept the invitation and on whom therefore the Lord pronounces His terrible and severe verdict: None of those men which were bidden shall eat of my supper. Supposing that were said of us, of us Christians who have received the invitation and who, as we say, are precisely the people professing to believe in God, in Jesus, and in the Bible? What then does it mean to accept or not accept the invitation? How can we put ourselves to the test to discover whether we are accepting it or not?

Our first and fundamental answer to this question must be: assuredly they do not accept the invitation who do not properly believe in it. Whoever does not believe in the future reality of the kingdom can also not embrace it and help to embody it.

Hence Jesus narrates this parable to us and the theme of my preaching to-day—not merely to you but also to myself—is the necessity to test ourselves and see whether we really believe in the coming of the kingdom. Do you believe in the infinite splendour of the future in the eternal kingdom of God, which must mark the end of all human history and of the individual human life according to the will of God? Do you believe that God invites you personally to His great supper? That is clearly the crucial question. There cannot be a more important question either in my life or in your life or in the life of anyone: do you believe that you personally are bidden and that the invitation means eternal communion with God and with the family of all mankind?

My friends, I cannot answer for you. What I can do and will now do is simply this: I will draw your attention somewhat to the *way in which and the reasons for which so many do not accept the invitation,* and thus I will point out the various symptoms in which a fundamental unbelief is manifested. Some say: this teaching of an eternal kingdom of God is too remote from my needs. I would certainly like to cherish a hope for the future but not for a future so distant. I would like to be able to entertain hopes for the life of the here and now, not simply for the life of eternity; hopes which are capable of realization in this world, not only in the world that is to come.

I have heard people who really want to be Christians say: eternal life does not interest me at all, I am interested only in this world. And then they generally attempt to distort the message of the eternal kingdom of God so that it becomes a message concerning the progress of good on this earth. Jack wants to know more than his master, Christians insist on knowing better than the Lord Jesus Christ Himself and His apostles who always when they speak of the kingdom of God mean the eternal kingdom, the life of the world to come.

But, such people usually add, is it not right and proper that we should concern ourselves chiefly with what is taking place and will take place on this earth? The Bible teaches us the opposite and experience suggests that the more men occupy themselves only with this world and its temporal interests, and do not believe in eternal life or turn away from it, so much the worse do things go even in this space-time world and its concerns. What we are experiencing to-day in the life of the individual and the life of humanity, of the nations and of the whole civilized world, is to be understood as the effect of a sort of *panic fear of the end*. Because men do not believe in eternal life therefore they suppose they must pack everything into their life in this world. For, they reason, afterwards there will probably be annihilation. And the result is that their reaction to this world takes one of two forms and often both together: the illusory dream of an earthly paradise and the despair of attaching any meaning whatsoever to life. The illusion of establishing an earthly paradise, which might also be described as utopianism, is one manifestation of the sickness of our time. Men insist on realizing these utopias at any cost, and since that cannot be done so easily they use violence in order forcibly to bring about their realization. That is the origin of the violence and tyranny so typical of our age. Once a great thinker said: "When men insist on creating paradise they create hell." That is true, and how profoundly true it is we are finding out to-day. The other possible result when men no longer believe in eternal life or cease to concern themselves about it, is *despair*. They then see nothing but meaninglessness in their life and in the life of humanity. Everything is being precipitated towards the abyss and the finality of death. There exists in fact to-day a philosophy of downright despair, which of course describes itself by other names, but the meaning of which in practice can be summed up in the terms: after all death comes at last and all is hastening towards the gulf of death. Hence life has no meaning and can only give rise to despair. This consequence flows from the fact that in Christianity itself the message of the great supper and of the eternal kingdom of God is no longer believed.

But unbelief and the refusal to follow up the invitation can also take a less obvious form. For instance, people say: I do indeed already believe in that truth but for the present and in my present circumstances other things are of greater importance to me. This course represents the *postponement of the invitation* until at some future date a convenient moment arrives. Here and now and under present circumstances one has other things to do and think about both in regard to thought and action. The great invitation remains so to speak in the background, just as in one's correspondence the most urgent letters are placed on top and the less urgent which can wait are shoved beneath, with the idea that they can be dealt with at some more convenient time. Do we not often act thus? Hence to every one of us the solemn warning comes to-day: do not act thus, do not postpone the matter, otherwise you might find it is too late. God sends the invitation to you to-day and wills that to-day you answer Him. Indeed He Himself has come to invite you: "Behold I stand at the door and knock. If anyone will open to me, I will go in and sup with him."

Let me illustrate what I mean by a story. Two neighbours have quarrelled and parted company for some reason or other. Then it occurs to one of them that this situation is just not right. He writes a letter to his former friend suggesting that they make peace. He receives no reply. Come now, he thinks, I must try again. "Let us make peace and resume our former friendly relations." Still no reply. Then the man decides one evening— it is a bitterly cold winter's night with howling wind and snow —to undertake the long journey to the other man's house on foot. He arrives panting, snowed up, and petrified with cold. He repeats by word of mouth his invitation. And now it begins to dawn on his neighbour that he has before him a real human being, frozen, drenched with snow, and panting. Now his heart melts and he takes the invitation seriously. Now he says Yes.

This neighbour is God. He has written to us many a letter and we have not answered Him. Finally He Himself has come to dwell as a poor man among men, as one who had not where to lay His head, finally as one who was slain on the cross because men refused to believe in His invitation. And yet in that hour the eyes of some were opened: such is the love of God towards us, so piercing is His invitation that we cannot now fail to say yes.

That, my friends, is the meaning of the Christmas message. That is the sense of the whole gospel of Jesus Christ the crucified. God repeats His invitation but this time not merely with a letter, getting up early and sending His prophets, this time He comes Himself to us as the crucified Saviour so that we may realize how serious He is about His message of peace. The Saviour in His parable alludes to the fact that the invited do not seriously pay attention and for various reasons decline. He is thinking of the Jews, most of whom declined. Of course the apostles too were Jews but they constituted a very small minority. The greater part of Jewry emphatically said no. But God will not allow Himself to be defeated by those who decline. When that happens He invites others. Jesus is alluding to the Gentiles, to whom the invitation goes when the Jews decline.

But for us this means: if *you Christians*, who for two thousand years have been in receipt of the invitation, fail to accept it, then it will go *to the heathen*. And that is the point which we want to bear particularly in mind on this missionary Sunday. What the Lord declared has been wonderfully fulfilled in our time too. The gospel of Jesus Christ and of His great supper has come to the heathen and comes constantly to them. But that also has happened which the parable teaches—they have accepted it—not all, of course, only a small percentage, but nevertheless it amounts already to many millions in all parts of the earth. And their acceptance of it has not been purely formal. What struck us particularly at the Amsterdam conference of world Churches was the fact that precisely the representatives of the so-called young Churches—the Churches in India, Africa, Indonesia and so on—sounded a clear note of joyful faith and hope in such a way as to give us the impression of a living, sincere and spirit-filled Christian life. The situation now is certainly no longer that which obtained in former ages of missionary activity, when the European and American Churches were the givers and those others the receivers. The page has turned or is in the process of turning; the new Churches are the givers and we the receivers. This revolution has at least begun, and—let us not forget—this has happened as a result of centuries of devoted and self-sacrificial missionary work. It is impossible to foresee what it will mean for the world and also for ourselves when the seed of the gospel will have borne fruit a hundredfold among these nations which have had to wait so long to hear the word, and now with such eagerness and longing seize upon their invitation to the great supper.

But the parable of the Lord reminds us of something else. There are also, *even among ourselves*, even at home, in so-called Christian Europe, heathen without number. Missionary work has therefore become an urgent necessity among ourselves, and in this respect too we can already say how often it happens that just those who previously knew nothing and wished to know nothing of Christ and His Church receive the word with an impressively keen faith, and how so often it is seen, just in their lives, that the man who really believes, really says yes to the invitation, is born again and becomes a new creature, since he now has a lively hope which fills him with joy unspeakable and lends to his life a seriousness of responsibility which formerly he did not know.

Jesus narrated the parable to the Jews who were living in the faith that they were the chosen people and that the kingdom of God belonged to them. We are the rightful heirs of the promise, they thought. Hence they rocked themselves in their complacent self-security, in the thought of having and possessing. Because of this saturation in self-security and self-righteousness they were not in a position to understand the message of Jesus. They considered Him to be a false Messiah and a blasphemer. Thus they crucified Him. That was their answer to the invitation which He brought to them personally in the name of God.

And now we Christians stand in the very same danger. We

think the gospel belongs to us and do not realize that its implications are universal. We have so often read but never really understood or believed that the first shall be last and the last first. From childhood you have heard the gospel preached, are confirmed, and go to church. Very well. But are you also quite so sure that you have accepted it? Christian baptism proves nothing other than that you were once bidden to the feast. It does not prove that you are following up the invitation. Your churchgoing, your Bible reading, your prayers—all that is very well; but even that does not show that you have really accepted the invitation. The Jews, too, read their Bible, went to the synagogue, and prayed. And yet most of them did not belong to the small number of those who accepted the invitation. The inviting is God's concern: it is the word of God's unfathomable and infinite grace going out to all and promising to all eternal life—the greatest thing that a man can hope for. But the appropriation of that message is our concern, the opening of the door, for God does not deny us the freedom of coming to Him.

But what are the *signs* by which we may discover whether or not we have accepted the word? The first sign is that shown by the publican whom God contrasts with the Pharisee; the one says: God be merciful to me a sinner, and because he was himself invited, all unworthy, he wishes to extend a welcome to all others and thus does not presume to set himself over against them as one who is righteous and can look down on the unbelieving, unrighteous, and heathen world. The second sign is this: that with joy and earnestness one looks forward to and deems nothing more important than the great consummation, the great feast of eternal communion with God in His kingdom; thus one becomes a man who orientates his life towards this eternal goal and lives in confident and joyful anticipation of it. And the third sign—which of course can only count along with the two others—is the effort to bring the gospel within the reach of others who in truth are not more unworthy than ourselves so that they too may be invited and prepared to receive the invitation.

The last sentence of the parable ("I tell you that none of those that were bidden shall taste of my supper") is not said to make us afraid but to incite us to serious self-examination and to jolt us out of our satiation and smugness and our tendency to postpone indefinitely our acceptance. Yet you never know how much more time you still have. Pull yourself together and utter a wholehearted joyful and confident Yes. Live henceforth in the glad certainty that all life and your life is pointing towards this glorious end. Live in the serious endeavour to equip yourself for the coming of that glorious time and to go forward to meet it.

ELECTION

Blessed be the God and Father of our Lord Jesus Christ, who hath blessed us with every spiritual blessing in the heavenly places in Christ: even as He chose us in Him before the foundation of the world, that we should be holy and without blemish before Him in love: having foreordained us unto adoption as sons through Jesus Christ unto Himself, according to the good pleasure of His will, to the praise of the glory of His grace, which He freely bestowed on us in the Beloved.

Eph. 1: 3–6

IN these opening verses of the Epistle to the Ephesians the apostle speaks about divine *election* which took place before the foundation of the world. This idea has become known to history as *predestination*. And the thought of predestination worries and depresses many men to-day. If everything is predetermined, they say, what is there left for us to do? What justification can there possibly be for all our decisions and efforts when everything has already been predestined from all eternity? Yes, they face this Biblical message in a mood as it were of deep disillusionment and almost despair, as though to say: now even the Bible is going to leave us in the lurch. We are already tired of hearing in every other quarter that what is to be will be, that we are enslaved and predetermined and all that affects us is fixed beforehand, and now the Bible adds its voice to these voices of the world and adds its confirmation to the idea of predetermination.

It is true that on all sides the thought presses upon us that there is no room for freedom but that things must shape themselves in accordance with inner necessity. There is, for example, the world view of *Marxist socialism*, the so-called materialistic theory of history, the content of which is just this—that the whole history of the world runs its course in obedience to a sort of natural process with the same irrevocable natural necessity as any series of natural phenomena. Once the air above us has taken on a particular condition as regards temperature, moisture and charge of electricity then there must needs be stormy weather. All that is unchangeable, it is the course of nature. But look, they say, it is precisely thus with the history of human life. That too unfolds itself according to laws of nature. There is no freedom, all is fate.

But we are affected more closely as persons by a similar doctrine which, originating in *natural science*, explains the effects of the laws of heredity. Every man is what he is destined to be by the mass of his inherited tendencies. Just as you can do nothing about it whether you are blond or dark, blue-eyed or black-eyed—you have inherited those features from your parents and grandparents and great-grandparents—so you cannot change your character. That too is inherited and determines your destiny for you, just as much as the colour of your hair and eyes. The idea that you are responsible for what you do, that you freely decide this or that and can choose your way yourself—all that is mere illusion. In reality everything was already predetermined in the moment when your father and mother gave you birth and thus the two hereditary complexes of your parents formed your individuality by their union.

These teachings to-day exercise an inescapable influence upon the minds of us all and induce the feeling that we are merely the playthings of powers against which we can do nothing and to which we can make no appeal. "That is how I am made", says a girl whom her mother scolds about something she ought not to have done. "I have not made myself. How can I help it when I have inherited from my father and mother this particular character?" It is as though such theories infected the very air we breathe and coursed through our veins. What is there to do about it? Let it work itself out as it will.

And now to crown all comes *the Bible* too with its teaching about predestination. Instead of helping us out of this fatalistic dilemma from its transcendent height it aggravates our problem and says: everything is predetermined by God. Every-

thing springs as it must from the divine counsels. You are merely a pawn which God moves as He will and the whole game
has been long planned in advance and the way in which it is to
work out decided. All has already been decided in God's eternal
plan. Do not imagine that you can modify that plan in any way.
Thus, from the standpoint of God, too, our situation is such that
we can do nothing, but everything comes about as it must,
whether we will or not. Hence there is no point in bending our
efforts and concentrating our thoughts and pulling ourselves together.

My friends, if you really read your Bibles and do not simply
allow yourselves to be, so to speak, hypnotized by the one word
predestination, then you will realize that the word of God
means, says, and wills, *something altogether different*. The word of
God does not support those who desire to persuade us out of
our sense of responsibility and the freedom which it necessarily
involves and to say to us "You can do nothing at all". To what
purpose otherwise would the word of God address us? Why
would God otherwise in the whole history of His self-revelation be at such pains to win the heart of man? Indeed, why
would God have gone to the extreme length of taking humanity upon Himself and become man to reveal to us His love
and His holiness if in spite of everything all is as it will be, and if,
after all, our decision and our opening of our hearts does not
count? In all this self-revealing action God is speaking with us
in order to draw us to His side. If everything turned out as it
must then God could really have spared Himself this trouble,
and it would have been a curiously fallacious manœuvre on
His part to act as if our decision for faith and obedience were
of any effect.

Neither, on the other hand, does the word of God declare to
us what a certain type of secular philosophy seeks to render
plausible: every one is the architect of his own fortunes. Thank
God that is not so. If my happiness were dependent on my own
powers of craftsmanship, then the prospects would really not
be good. If primarily the deciding factor is what *I* am able to
effect and the adequacy of *my own* resources, then my prospects for the future would certainly not be bright. If all depends

on me, then of course I need no God and no Saviour. Then God simply plays the part of a distributor of rewards who, after the struggle of life is over, gives to each one his mark and the prize which he deserves, while in the drama of life itself he would leave each one of us to flounder all alone and would be simply a spectator of the way in which we acquit ourselves and fashion our fortunes. When we read the Bible this point of view finds even less support. If our freedom, our personality, and our own power of decision may not be excluded, still less can we eliminate God's decision and Person, God's activity and power of operation. Hence neither are we a mere pawn in the game of fate nor is God a mere commending or condemning spectator and distributor of rewards at the conclusion of our life-struggle and life performance. Obviously the truth is of a very different character from either of these solutions which man himself is able to give as an interpretation of the meaning of his life. Let us hear the word of Paul in regard to this matter.

"Blessed be the God and Father of our Lord Jesus Christ, who hath blessed us with every spiritual blessing in the heavenly places in Christ."

Thus what is here in question is God, His action and His gift. And, indeed, all praise and thanks to God, that is the primary thing. Our life is in better hands than our own. There flows into our life from God something which we cannot with all our pursuit and struggle achieve for ourselves. This power which flows into our life from God above is here described as: *spiritual blessing from the heavenly places.* And this blessing from heaven may be summed up in a single word, in a single name: *Christ.* In Him something has been enacted towards us men and on our behalf which is not within our power of accomplishment, but comes down to us from above just as the rain falls from heaven on the parched earth and makes it bring forth and bud. Just as little as the earth can bear fruit without the rain from heaven, so little can man—I or you or anyone—truly bear fruit of human virtue apart from what has come into our lives from God in Jesus Christ.

We men, and quite specially we modern men, are constantly inclined to think that by our own intrinsic virtue we can be good, upright and human men; if only we are left to ourselves, then all will be well. We do not at all, in fact, believe that without God we cannot be truly human. We suppose on the contrary that within ourselves we have the resources of true humanism. In reality, however, the fact is that the more we delude ourselves into thinking that we are independent of God, the more certainly we degenerate and sink to a sub-human level. It is that, of course, which to-day we are experiencing in a greater measure than ever before. In those states where human society and especially its rulers have emancipated themselves completely from the authority of God, as whole peoples and states have done to an unprecedented extent, then there emerges a dehumanization to which there is no parallel in previous history. With every step which separates man from God there springs up inhumanity, and the truly human element disappears from life.

This recognition is a primary truth which we apprehend through Jesus Christ. Through and in His life God has shown us what *true humanity* and the meaning of life is. Secondly, in Him God has disclosed the fact that we can realize this truly human meaning of life only through fellowship with God. The specifically human is *love*. But love is the very being of God. Whoever wills to dwell in love must perforce dwell in God. Whoever lives in isolation from God and wills to do so loses love and therewith the whole meaning of his life. But in Jesus Christ God has given us more than this mere recognition. He has further shown us that we are all involved in a way of life which implies the loss of this essential meaning, in fact, that if nothing else comes from the initiative of God we are beyond all hope of rescue, heading for disaster. Already our communion with God is dissolved and we could not, even if we so wished, re-establish ourselves in life-giving fellowship with Him. This destructive severance of our communion with God the Bible calls sin. And this latter reality lurks in us all like a malignant growth which, unless the transcendent One intervenes, consumes our vitality and health increasingly.

But with Jesus Christ God has gone further. He has not only disclosed the danger of our condition; He has intervened like a surgeon who removes the growth. Jesus Christ has overcome the isolating force which separates us from God and precludes the possibility of our communion with Him, so that our fellowship with Him is restored so soon as we allow the initiative of Jesus to have its effect in our lives and yield ourselves to Him who reconciles us with God.

It is this divine action which in the Bible is called the grace of God in Jesus Christ. And to accept this grace, to allow the redeeming work of Jesus Christ to control our lives, is there called faith. In so far as Jesus Christ reconciles us with God through our faith in God's gracious pardon, true humanity begins to grow in us again. We again participate in the love of God from which we were alienated by sin. Then the spiritual blessing of God like the fructifying rain of heaven can pour into our lives and make all things new in them. Thus God has shed abroad in our hearts His grace and love, and again and again does so as long as we remain in that communion with Him which Jesus Christ has restored, and never again divorce ourselves from it.

It is in this context of thought that we must view what the Bible here says about eternal election. *God has chosen us in Him before the foundation of the world that we might be holy and blameless before Him.* What does this mean? God has created the world because He wills to share His life and to create an eternal fellowship of spirits. God is love. He wills to create that He might impart to His creatures His love and His eternal life. Such is the will of God from which the world took its origin. This will precedes creation just as the plan of the architect precedes the building of the house. As he has planned, so he builds. As God has planned, so He has built. And in this plan not only is man in general included—man to whom God wishes and is able to impart Himself in a quite special way, for the simple reason that only a being who appreciates love can return love. Still more, God has included in this plan every individual being whom He creates; even you and me. You—the individual—are woven into God's eternal pattern. You do not only exist because your parents have given you birth. You exist because God willed you to exist before the foundation of the world.

4

Does not this seem too presumptuous an idea to be convincing? Could it really be that the eternal God, the Creator of the whole universe, should so care for me the individual and attach such importance to me, that He had me in view when He created the world? Is it not unreasonable to believe so much about ourselves? I certainly agree that it would be out of all sense and reason to think so if the thought originated in our minds. In fact no man on his own initiative would arrive at such an audacious conception. But it is not presumptuous to believe it when God Himself declares it to us in Jesus Christ. Through Him He discloses to each one of you: you were an eternal thought in my mind before the worlds were created. Consider, God thinks of men not merely in general terms. God thinks always in terms of the concrete person. Generalities are for us a necessary expedient because we are unable to grasp such a manifold of concrete particulars. But God can do so. Before His countenance we all stand with our name and face and He knows each one of us infinitely better than we know ourselves.

But we stand in the light of His countenance not merely as we are in our present condition. In the eternal design of God we are not the sinful, weak, frail and mortal men whom now we empirically are, but such as bear the stamp and the image of Jesus Christ, His eternal Son. He has designed us according to the model of Him who is the express image of His substance. Just as the head of a motor factory has designed a 1955 model for the year 1955 and then proceeds to the execution of his plan, so God has designed a model of true humanity in the man Jesus Christ who appeared on earth. This Jesus Christ is the plan of God in creation for each one of us. This archetype prepared by God from all eternity before the world was created has been actualized up to now only in one exemplar—in Jesus Christ, the true man, who is also the revelation of the true God. But we in our present condition are very different from this true man. We are sinful, frail men—the prey of death. Yet God has sent us His Son in order to declare to us that in spite of our sin He cleaves to His plan; that He still sees us and wills to see us as He did before the foundation of the world; as true men whom He has destined to be like unto His Son.

Hence whoever believes in Jesus sees in Him the pattern of his own life. Not as he at present is, but as God has envisioned and willed him to be eternally. Not as a 1955 model but in the light of the archetypal true man Jesus Christ, beloved from all eternity. Hence the believer knows the meaning of that word: elected before the foundation of the world. Elected does not mean predetermined so that we would be simply pawns pushed hither and thither by God without our being able to do anything about it, but elected means *eternally beloved of God in Jesus Christ His Son*. Thus we need not be afraid of this Biblical message about election and need not suppose that it implies the destruction of our freedom. On the contrary, this word election is the eternal, true and sure ground on which we may stand and on the basis of which we may be certain of the love of God and of our belonging eternally to Him.

But the Bible has not a word to say about that terrible doctrine which may be described as *dual* predestination. It represents a fearful, I might almost say blasphemous, misunderstanding. We could never suppose that, as Calvin declared, God has eternally created two types of humanity, the one appointed to eternal life, the other to eternal damnation. There is a way of life and a way of death. That idea cannot be eliminated from the Bible. But the implication of this statement is as follows: the way of life is the way on which we allow ourselves to be placed by faith in Jesus Christ, the way of death is the way which runs contrary to Jesus Christ and in which we walk when we reject Jesus Christ. Whoever walks in the way of Jesus Christ may understand the truth of the word: elected from all eternity. And this way is open to each one of us. None is excluded; the invitation goes out to each of us. But the invitation involves also a decision and indeed a serious one, the only quite serious decision of our lives, the decision to walk in the way which leads to life and away from that which leads to death and destruction.

This is the crucial issue at stake for each one of us; for you and for me. But if you enquire what happens in that case to those who make the wrong decision, allow me to say something which applies to the whole revelation of God in His word.

God speaks to *you* that *you* may make the right decision. But God does not satisfy our curiosity as to what happens about other men who do not decide for Christ. What will be the ultimate fate of other men is not your concern; we may not and are not to know that, except in so far as we must realize that it is our duty not only ourselves to remain loyal to the way of Jesus, but as far as possible to help others to find the way that leads to life. It is not the consequence of our superior merit that we ourselves have found this way. We have not come to it because we are better than other people. It is the grace of God which has set our feet in that way. For this reason we must always hope of every man, however much he may be alienated from God, that his eyes will yet be opened and that even yet he too may decide for Christ.

When we begin to puzzle our brains and to wish to know more than we should, to know why God gives His grace to one and not to another, then we hit upon this dreadful thought of dual predestination. But we are not meant in this life to concern ourselves with these curious enquiries. God's word is not spoken to us for that purpose. Revelation is given to us for fruitful, not for unfruitful, purposes. Such brooding is profitless, but faith in Jesus Christ bears fruit in good works. And that brings me to the last point which the text and the Gospel in general teaches us. You are elected in Jesus Christ *to walk in His way and not in your own*, hence to obey Him and not to do your own will. You may and you must live as one who is eternally beloved of God, on whom God bestows His love and from whom therefore is expected active love towards other men. "If a man say he loves God but does not love his brother and seeks his own, he is a liar." We are elected by God in Jesus Christ in order, as it says here, *to be holy and blameless before Him*. Whoever belongs to Jesus Christ must also live in harmony with His mind, and not as one who disgraces Him, and instead of doing the will of God does his own will. Hence it is said in the second epistle of Timothy: "He who names the name of the Lord must abstain from all injustice." Our obedience to this command of God in so far as is possible is the necessary consequence of the fact that our feet are set in the way which Jesus has prepared for us. For "He died for all, that they which live should no longer live unto themselves but unto Him who died for them." Let us ponder that thought and keep it well in our minds. Let us pray for and struggle to attain this obedience. For in this regard it will be seen whether we have really entered into the way of Jesus Christ, which is the way of life.

THE FOLLY AND SCANDAL OF THE CROSS

For the word of the Cross is to them that are perishing foolishness; but unto us which are being saved, it is the power of God. For it is written, I will destroy the wisdom of the wise, and the prudence of the prudent will I reject. Where is the wise? Where is the scribe? Where is the disputer of this world? hath not God made foolish the wisdom of the world? For seeing that in the wisdom of God the world through its wisdom knew not God, it was God's good pleasure through the foolishness of the preaching to save them that believe. Seeing that Jews ask for signs, and Greeks seek after wisdom: but we preach Christ crucified, unto Jews a stumbling block, and unto Gentiles foolishness; but unto them that are called, both Jews and Greeks, Christ the power of God and the wisdom of God.

I Cor. I: 18–24

WE live in the age of scientific knowledge. If humanity of to-day feels itself to be so fundamentally different from that of former ages it is due above all to the influence of *science*. It is, in fact, truly astonishing to see the changes that have been wrought in the last two centuries and still more in the last fifty years. In $2\frac{1}{2}$ hours we can now fly to London. We turn a knob on a tiny box and hear a speech by the American President in California. Illnesses which formerly almost certainly meant death have become harmless. By means of the telescope we have penetrated the unfathomable depths of stellar space and by means of the microscope we have pierced the secrets of the infinitely small. What wonder is it if men of to-day cherish a boundless confidence in science and expect of it what in former ages they looked for from religion and God? The wisdom of this world has become a mighty thing which we can no longer despise. On the other hand, in proportion as the respect for science and for human wisdom has increased, the esteem for Biblical divine revelation has diminished. "We no longer need any religion because we now have science" was a dictum which some time ago could be heard in a big students' assembly in England. Formerly we prayed if it thundered and lightened, but to-day we trust in the lightning-conductor. Formerly we prayed for God's blessing on the growth of the seed, but to-day, following scientific instructions, we insert into the soil a certain chemical material which guarantees growth. It really does look as if faith in God belonged to the childhood of humanity and that we have superseded it as we have grown up by the aid of science. Is that really the case, my friends?

Yes, can we honestly say that we have arrived at such a glorious age? Have we by means of knowledge and human wisdom overcome the great enemies of human life? war between the nations, strife between races, classes and parties, divorce and family feuds? Have we to-day fewer cares and less anxiety? Have we overcome the power of death and got rid of the feeling of senselessness and despair? Are there fewer men to-day than formerly who cannot fit themselves into life and in despair commit suicide? One need only ask these questions in order to see that in reality the opposite is the case. Of what use is it if nations of east and west can speak to each other on the telephone if what they say to each other is nothing but the mutual threat of war? The drawing together of nations by means of technics, from which so much was hoped a hundred or fifty years ago, has hardly become a reality. The growing upward curve of suicide statistics hardly suggests that humanity of to-day has become happier or better. We do not say all this in order to depreciate human science but to remind ourselves of the fact that it does not touch the central problems of human living. Moreover, many scientists of to-day have become acutely conscious of this. They have come to realize that we need something else besides knowledge if we are to introduce meaning and order into our human relationships. But this other thing that is needed—must it be precisely the gospel of Jesus Christ the crucified?

Must it be nothing other than that message of which the apostle declares that it is *folly in the sight of the wise*? Should it not rather be a higher wisdom which is especially illuminating to the highly cultured and the wise of this world?

It is no accident that there are many cultured people among us to-day, precisely among those who have realized that mere secular science is not sufficient and that we need something more lofty, who are turning to other religions and not to the Christian faith. I am not thinking now of those conceited intellectuals who always want to be different and are for ever running after something new, and for whom therefore the Christian message, which is not at all new, is not good enough. I am thinking of serious-minded seekers after truth who, so they tell us, can make nothing of Christianity and for whom, on the other hand, Buddhism or Indian religion in general or the mysticism of Persia and China or something of that sort seems to supply precisely what they need.

Hence let us ask the question why it is that Paul describes the gospel as a folly and a scandal, and why the true doctrine of God must be precisely of such a character that worldly wisdom feels repelled by it? The passage from which our text is taken contains towards its conclusion the sentence: "so that no flesh may glory before God . . ." and concludes with the word of Jeremiah: "Whosoever glories let him glory in the Lord." *Self-praise before God*—it is that which is pierced and annihilated by the gospel of Jesus Christ. The wisdom of this world gives man occasion to be proud of his own achievement. Even the Jewish religion with its legalistic piety comes down in the last resort to the fact that it is still man who must do the decisive thing in order to win the good pleasure of God. This applies still more to oriental and mystical religions. The latter do not mortify man, they do not expose human sin, but by-pass it. But the message of the cross proclaims to us, to each one of us, even the best and most pious: You are a sinner, you are in a wrong relationship with God and hence with your fellow man also. You are seeking yourself. You desire to gain recognition for yourself. You wish to appear clever, and to attain the highest by means of your own intrinsic powers. You do not perceive that everything that you do, even the best, comes under this condemnation.

But why, you ask, must it be that in Christian doctrine so much ado is always made about human sin? Is there then nothing more important and better to be said than the fact that we are sinners? My friends, so long as we talk thus—and in a sense we are always thinking in these terms—we have not realized the depth of our own need and of the need of humanity, and thus the root of all that evil from which man suffers despite all his progress. It is just this recognition which is in question: in my inmost being I have gone astray: I am godless, loveless, self-seeking, God-escaping. It is not the fact that sin consists merely in those obvious weaknesses and vices which everyone condemns as sinful and evil, which, however, do not constitute our true being and with which, to a very large extent, we ourselves can deal. No, sin—the corruption of our nature—lies much deeper and is manifest even when we are occupied with the highest and holiest things. Luther in a very pregnant saying describes man as a heart that is turned in upon itself—a heart that in the last analysis always loves itself and not God and the neighbour. This vitiating characteristic betrays itself even in our beneficent actions, in our noblest moral efforts, nay, more, even in our piety and prayer. Always there is disclosed the heart that is self-centred, that ego that seeks itself, and has a good conceit of itself and secretly longs for praise and recognition. Ethics, philosophy, the highest wisdom of the world, even the re-ligions of the east, know nothing of just this, of this depth of perversity, of this sin which gnaws at the root of our being, of this poison which corrupts all that we are and do, even the highest and the best. Hence they do not attack this evil at its root and, in the last resort, cannot remove it. They effect only a superficial alleviation.

But the message of the cross goes to the root of our ills, and it alone can cure them radically. Just for that reason it spells folly and scandal. How does it do so? In the Bible as a whole, and already in the Old Testament, the point always is that man does not find a way to God but that God comes to man. What is in question is not the recognition of higher worlds, not a vision which man might acquire by a special technique of mysticism. We do not hear in the Bible of any practice of mystical introspection, of otherworldliness, of cultivating the interior life, with a view to reaching ultimately the divine ground of the soul. It is not a question of man's own perform-ances and exercises as a result of which he might hope to be-come pious and well-pleasing to God. All that is man's way to God and in the last analysis self-praise. The central point is that God has mercy on man who is so stuck fast in the mire—if I may be pardoned the expression—that he cannot help himself. That is the meaning of the story which begins with Abraham and Moses and proceeds to the prophets, including that greatest of the prophets, who tells us of the servant of God who suffers for our sakes and burdens himself with our guilt.

And so at last God comes to us in Jesus Christ, the Saviour of sinners, who sups with Zacchaeus, the notorious tax-gatherer, collaborationist, and traitor, and who is therefore dubbed the friend of publicans and sinners, and who at last goes His way to the cross in the knowledge that He must not shrink from the uttermost sacrifice in order to consummate God's coming to man. Behold the man!—the servant of God who suffers for our sakes and bears our sins and so effaces them that they can no longer place a barrier between God and man. He has paid your debts. He has overcome the distance which separated the holy God from you, the unholy and miserable sinner, so that now there is no more any wall of partition blocking our access to God. For you and in your room He has suffered the criminal's death, the accursed death which you should have suffered, so that you may realize this truth: "God so loved the world that He gave His only begotten Son, that whosoever believeth in Him should not perish but have everlasting life." Thus in Jesus Christ God Himself has cleared out of the way all that you yourself could not do, so that nothing now hinders you in your approach to God. He has done so, that now you might be reconciled with Him through what He alone has done, might believe in His love and live by the power of His overflowing mercy and forgiving grace. All that God Himself has done. You have done nothing at all in this work of grace. All will be forgiven you by God's pure gift; not on the basis of your own deserving and achievement. All the praise for this work of love falls on God alone—nothing at all on you. "Whoever glories let him glory in the Lord, who has become to us righteousness, sanctification, and healing."

That, my friends, is the foolish and scandalizing message of the cross. It appears foolish to us because there is here no talk of enlightenment which we might gain through thinking, philosophizing, or cultural development. It is scandalous or offensive, a stone of stumbling, repellent, because it leaves all to the operation of God and assigns to us no part except that of accepting the gift. We now know why so many refuse to hear this message and, as they say, can make neither head nor tail of it. The man for whom his reasoning power furnishes the supreme criterion of truth cannot believe that truth exists which does not flow from thinking, and from his own intellectual activity; truth which we cannot, by our own powers of recognition, apprehend, or by our powers of reason demonstrate, truth which does not dovetail into our own systems of thought and knowledge and which lies entirely beyond the reach of our capacities. All this so clashes with our pride in our unaided faculties of reason and our cultural enlightenment that there are only two alternatives open to us: either to reject it as nonsensical fantasy and myth, as a hangover from primitive ways of thought, or to put aside our intellectual complacency and to accept it as the gift of God in childlike sincerity, as the simplest old woman might do.

Still more serious than the folly is the *offensiveness* of it. It is no accident that Paul says it is folly to the Greeks but to the Jews a scandal. The Greeks seek after wisdom. But the Jews desire by their good works to merit the favour of God. Perhaps you yourselves have felt somewhat the repugnance of this message while I have been preaching. Has not the thought come to you: Well, what then remains for us to do? It is really too easy to accept merely a gift and to leave everything to God's operation. What room is there in that case for our own exertions, our own sense of responsibility? Can such a message have any other effect but to make men frivolous and idle? The Jews thought just so and just for that reason they rejected the message of Jesus Christ, and also in fact Jesus Christ Himself.

The fact that He was the friend of publicans and sinners made them indignant. Such frivolity, they said, is unpardonable. He must be a blasphemer.

Look, once again, at the revolt of our natural pride, this time not the pride of reason, but pride in our moral powers and in our determination to get things done for ourselves. And here again there is only one of two courses open to us: either to reject this frivolous doctrine of sole and sufficient grace, or, on the other hand, to surrender our moral pride and our pride in our own powers of achievement and to say in all humility: Yes, Lord, Thou alone canst put me in the right way and reconcile me with Thyself. All that I myself can do is actuated by the motives of a false and deceitful heart. Thou alone art the author of good and dost grant it freely without any merit or achievement on our part and without conditions, except one: that we accept it. And so I decide to accept it and I thank Thee from the bottom of my heart. Such is the way of faith. And under the impact of this faith all pride in reason collapses, all glorying ceases, except one kind: the praise of God who has accomplished all this for us in Jesus Christ.

In conclusion let me consider two questions. How must we regard human wisdom and knowledge in the context of this kind of faith? All knowledge is right and good and necessary in its place and within its limits. It is right for us to research and to learn. God has not given us our intelligence in vain. He does not want us to become illiterate barbarians because we have faith. But we must realize that all our vaunted knowledge is worldly and human and therefore cannot help us in the deepest needs and distresses of human living. Knowledge is only to be repudiated when it becomes a religion, when man thinks that thereby God becomes superfluous or that it exposes God as illusory. It is this superstition and arrogance to which science gives birth that is to be rejected, not science itself.

Secondly: What is the position with regard to our own exertions and our own responsibilities? Consider once more what it is that God bestows upon us. He imparts to us His love, communion with Himself, and the fact that sin, which causes the deepest, most inward separation from Him, is done away. How could the man who really appropriates that gift become frivolous and irresponsible? Can one really receive the love of God without henceforth living in the strength of that love? I know very well from my own experience that even truly believing Christians are not saints in the sense that they do no more wrong. But that is only so because we again and again slip away from what Jesus Christ bestows upon us, are unfaithful to Him and lapse from our communion with Him. In proportion as we evermore allow ourselves to be anchored by faith in the love of God, we hardened sinners become transformed: boasting ceases. Arrogance and self-righteousness vanish. The latter are panzer armour which separates us as nothing else does from God and our neighbour. No sin cuts us off so effectively from God and our fellow men as the sin of pride. That is the root of all sins—the magnifying of the ego. Whoever stands in faith and constantly receives the grace of God, opening himself to its power, finds that this opaque ego is shattered and this arrogance dissolved.

Hence we are not anxious lest faith should not achieve the effects proper to it in the renewal of our lives. "Let us love Him, for He has first loved us."

YOUR REASONABLE SERVICE

I beseech you therefore, brethren, by the mercies of God, to present your bodies a living sacrifice, holy, acceptable to God, which is your reasonable service. And be not fashioned according to this world: but be ye transformed by the renewing of your mind, that ye may prove what is the good and acceptable and perfect will of God.

Rom. 12: 1–2

IN this exhortation of the apostle it is a question of the service of God. But not of the divine service which we are celebrating here to-day. Does the apostle suggest then that this is not the true service of God? Certainly not. The problem arises, then, how these two modes of the service of God are related to each other—that about which the apostle is preaching and this which we are performing here. When we meet together, as now, to hear the word of God and to respond to that word by our prayers and hymns and spiritual songs of praise, we are engaging in a service of God which is the background and presupposition for that other type of service. Here we are reminded of the fact that we are God's servants, and why we are so, and that in this relationship of service to God we are linked together as one community which serves.

Many modern men who profess belief in Christianity have no understanding for this sort of meeting together for worship —for what we are accustomed to describe as *public worship*. It does not appeal to me or help me, they say. They would prefer to read the Bible in private or switch on the radio and listen to a broadcast sermon, and they consider the practice of going to church as something outmoded and superfluous—a mere pious custom. That attitude is perhaps not simply their fault; for our public worship is not sufficiently an expression of the fact that here the community of Jesus Christ is assembled in reality and as His body accomplishes something. We should to a much greater extent be able to make every individual in church feel that in this act he has some part to play, that the worship of God is his affair, and not merely that of the parson while the congregation is relegated to the position of an audience. Our divine services are much in need of reform. But that is not the chief reason why people of this sort do not wish to take part in them. The reason lies at a much deeper level: they no longer understand that it is a question of a communal action of the assembling in fellowship of those who belong to Jesus Christ and who through Him are a communion of members knit together in one indivisible whole.

In fact we too who still to a large extent go regularly to church do not clearly realize this. We are not here assembled as in a concert auditorium to listen to a great soloist, nor in order, each one for himself, to get some help in the living of his daily life. We are together here in order that in fellowship with each other we may praise God, and in fellowship so assimilate His word that we come to realize this: that this divine Word makes us no longer a mere chance assembly of individuals but an integral whole, a people of God, a communion centred in Jesus Christ. Certainly our public worship lacks much which might have the effect of bringing home to us more forcibly this consciousness of unity and community. But even so, even with all its defects, our divine service can and should bring home to us the fact that although we may enter the church as individuals we do not leave it as such, but as a fellowship in Christ, spiritually united with those who have with us heard the Word and prayed and sung praises—nay, more, united with all those who throughout the earth perform this worship and in the name of Jesus Christ form a unity in contrast with the rest of humanity, the unity of the members of the body of Christ, the people of Christ, the people of God. Sunday worship does not exist merely for the individual so that he may hear God's word and become illuminated and strengthened by it. It exists in order to bring vividly to our consciousness the fact that we thus belong together. Individualization, the withdrawal into solitude, is just

63

what God does not will. The flight into our solitariness, the "I prefer to be by myself", or "no one is interested in me"—God is against this proud and melancholy isolation of the self. Christ has come in order to put an end to this atomization. If you are alone and proudly prefer to be by yourself, God wishes to teach you otherwise that you may no longer be proud to be alone. If you are alone because you think that no one takes any interest in you, then God wills to give you a jolt and tell you, "*I* am very much concerned about you. You are not alone and hence you belong to the inner life of my people."

You all belong to each other in one great family as brothers are one. That is one point, and the other is this: that by nature we wish to live unto ourselves each one unto himself. And this is reflected in our approach to divine worship. Have you not often said: the sermon has taught me nothing. But whether the sermon appeals to you is not the main point: the decisive thing is whether *you are offering yourself to God*.

We must not live unto ourselves, we do not belong to ourselves but we belong to God. And it is this awareness which should come to each one of us in every act of public worship when its spirit is the right one: we should thereby be shaken out of our solitariness and our desire to be alone, and our attitude should be changed to one of being unto God; and this should happen in proportion as we experience the being for each other and with each other.

And that is the essential import of the text: *our whole life is to be a service of God*. Our life must express this one theme: I am not a master but a servant. Consider, that is the deepest reason why so many refuse to know anything of the Gospel; they refuse to hear a message which calls them to service, they insist on ruling. They do not wish to minister but to be ministered unto. They do not wish to obey but to command and to do what pleases them. Such is the bent of our natural will, to be master, to be free, to govern. The whole history of modern humanity is characterized by this struggle for freedom. To be free and to be able to control nature by means of science and technics, to be free from human rulers of any kind but also to be free from what transcends us and places limits on the exercise of our will. Freedom is the great solution to man's problems offered by modern civilization. But this development leads ultimately to the opposite result: namely, servitude. And because man wishes above all things to be free he has rid himself of God in the process of shedding all that transcends him and limits his freedom. If there is a God, then I cannot be free; I must obey. But I insist on being free above all things, therefore I do not recognize the existence of God. That is the deepest reason for atheism and godlessness. We do away with God, we declare that God is dead and proclaim that religion is ignorant superstition and opium for the people. Our slogan is freedom, and at the very moment when this doctrine for the first time becomes the fundamental law of a state, the totalitarian state emerges by which each individual becomes a slave of state machinery. We wanted freedom and instead we got slavery. Why so? Because God has so made us that we cannot be free except in so far as we are the servants of God. If each man is free, unconditionally free, if each wishes to rule, the final result is the tyranny of those who are able to establish rule over the rest. True freedom is only possible in the service of God. If you wish to be free then serve God. Only when your life is a true service of God, can you be a truly free man.

How do you know this? I hear you ask. I will tell you how I know it. It is the insight which our Lord Jesus Christ has given us and has expressed in His own life. "The Son of Man has not come to be ministered unto but to minister and to give His life a ransom for many." That is not merely a word which Jesus has spoken, but it is what His whole life expresses. It is that by which we may know that He is true man. His life is a *truly free* life because it is a *genuine service of God*. Of Him it is true, and of Him alone it is completely true, that He gave His body and His life to be a living holy sacrifice well-pleasing to God; He lived in the form of a servant, as He made it plain to His disciples on that last evening when He washed their feet, performing the most menial of duties. In that service and sacrifice not only does He reveal to us what true human life is, but also the mystery of the Godhead. There He reveals Himself not only as true man but also as true God. In that reversal of the natural human desire to

be master in the sacrifice of Jesus on the cross, the secret of
divine mercy is disclosed to us.

"I beseech you by the mercy of God . . ." thus the apostle begins his exhortation about the true service of God. We do not
know of ourselves that true freedom can only be realized in
obedience to God. And not only do we not come to that recognition of ourselves; even though we knew it we should not be
able to carry it out in our own strength. For the ambitious impulse to rule is too strong in us. One cannot quite simply expect
people to view their lives in terms of service rather than the
exercise of power. That is contrary to our nature or rather it is
contrary to our present sinful nature. In fact that is precisely the
nature of original sin—that we wish to rule rather than serve
God, to be master ourselves and do our own will. What is
needed is a transformation of our inmost desires, of the very
life-impulse itself which is naturally bent on ruling rather than
on serving. How could we by our own efforts extinguish this
impulse, or rather how could we redirect the libido from a false
into a true channel? Who can so refashion our hearts that they
no longer point to ourselves but to God?

Obviously we cannot do that of ourselves. We cannot be
both the anvil and the hammer. Our impotence in this connexion as opposed to God's power and action in Jesus Christ—
that is the whole theme of the Epistle to the Romans. Consider,
that is what Paul wishes to say to us: you cannot in your own
strength enter on the true path of life. What you undertake by
your own initiative and capacity, your own works—all that is
vitiated by its self-centred character. In all these endeavours you
are seeking yourself—crudely or finely, secretly or openly. It is
clear that you cannot do otherwise. That you necessarily always
do what is perverse because you are essentially self-seeking—
that is what the Bible calls sin and you are so deeply involved in
that sinfulness by reason of your self-seeking nature that you
are in no position to change matters. But look, a man appeared
on this earth for whom things were otherwise; a man who in
fact did what he promised to do: viz. devote his life wholly to
God. If now you link yourself to Him and in His countenance
recognize your own perversity and accept the divine mercy and

love so disclosed—look, your own heart will then be melted and remoulded and reorientated from an egocentric to a theocentric direction. In so far as you love the God who addresses you in Jesus Christ and speaks to you in the cross of His dear Son, will your own will be transformed from its self-centred character into a God-centred character.

Such is the theme of Paul in the eleven chapters of the epistle which precede our text. He presupposes that we have understood all this, that we have recognized Christ the crucified as the revelation of God and of the true nature of man, that we believe in Him. Then he continues: "And now I exhort you by the mercies of God to offer your bodies as a living and holy *sacrifice*, well-pleasing to God."

Religion at all times has been concerned with sacrifice. This universal fact implies that man has always had some dim surmise of the true nature of his existence. He knows that he is obliged to offer sacrifices to God. But this sacrificial religion has also something about it that is foolish and irrational. As if God wanted gifts from us, whether it be bullocks or rams or flowers and fruit. God wants only *one* sacrifice—that of *ourselves*. In this alone consists our reasonable service—that we present ourselves as a living sacrifice to Him. But it is just this that we cannot do. Well, says Paul, *now* you can do this, *now* you are no longer such as live as though they belonged to themselves but as though they belonged to God through Jesus Christ. He has set your feet in a new path of life. So now strive to advance in this new direction.

I will once again refer to an analogy which I have previously used to illustrate this point. Jesus Christ is for us what the turnplate is to the steam engine. The engine cannot turn of itself in order to get on to the right rails. But it can run on the turntable which sets it in the right direction.

So it is with regard to Christ. Surrender yourself to Jesus Christ and He will revolutionize your life away from the false, self-centred, self-seeking ambition to rule and into the opposite direction of the service of God. Naturally as a result of this transformation or revolution we come to walk in a path of life which is opposed to the aims of the world. Do not be surprised about this, Paul tells us. Men will think you mad, the more you live in loyalty to the way of Christ. And indeed you have reversed your direction, but remember you have been switched from the wrong direction which leads to destruction to the right direction which leads to life. In fact, when we look at life from the angle of Christ it is the activities and the aims of the world which seem to us to be truly mad, and not only the purposes of the world surrounding us but also our own unsanctified purposes: whatever we do in so far as we abandon Christ and give way to our own natural wishes and thoughts. The true service of God consists just in the fact that we ever and again allow ourselves to be diverted from our own instinctive aims into fidelity to the will of Christ.

When we do that, then it comes to pass that our life becomes a veritable service of God. What a remarkable idea this is—*that our lives should consist in the worship of God*, that every day should be as sacred as divine service in church, that my life should sound a hymn of praise to God, should express unceasing thanksgiving and a constant awareness of the presence of Him who has created us. When you are surly, unpleasant, envious, overcritical, then you can be sure that you are running on your own lines.

Allow yourself to be changed from the self-seeking to the God-seeking direction. How wonderfully free life becomes when it is placed at the service of God! And how foolish is the opinion that there is something base about service and that to obey is less worthy than to command! On the contrary, the man who serves is the true nobleman and the man who obeys is the truly free man. Let us be honest with ourselves: at first it seems to us again and again unnatural, in fact senseless, to wish to serve rather than rule; to obey rather than to be emancipated. We must constantly remember all that it has cost God in His Son in order to banish from ourselves this supposed wisdom. The foolish and, to our own way of thinking, the scandalous message of the cross is the sole means by which we can learn and win for ourselves the wisdom of God and therewith the truth about our own life.

Only when our lives are thus revolutionized by God Himself

are we in a position to know what day by day and hour by hour God wills with us. The true service of God is no longer just a question of a law which we simply apply by rote and as a result of which we would always know beforehand the will of God. God is a living God and the Holy Ghost is a spirit of freedom. Whoever stands in the service of this Lord can never simply know beforehand what he is to do. He must ever and again wait upon God to know His will. Like officers and soldiers he must daily await and receive the order of the day issued by the supreme commander. The life of a man who has determined to live in the service of God is a life which does not develop according to a fixed pattern and a previously known law. It is day by day full of surprises.

In practice that means that every day we must do two things. We must ever remember the mercy of God, ever place ourselves on the turn-table which redirects us out of our own selfish lines on to the ways of God. And secondly: every day we must in the stillness listen to God to learn His will for the present hour, with its quite concrete and urgent tasks which face us.

Only so will there come about a unity between our Sunday worship and our weekday routine. Let us not neglect the divine service of Sunday, so that in communion with each other we are again made radioactive by the hearing of the Word of God and with each other and through each other learn to recognize and feel ourselves to be a people of the Lord. And let us then every morning each one in his privacy repeat what we have done in common on Sundays, and so link ourselves to God in our own individual lives, that as individuals we remain and prove ourselves to be members of His great world-wide Church.

PERSEVERANCE IN TRIAL

Because thou didst keep the word of my patience, I also will keep
thee from the hour of trial, that hour which is to come upon the
whole world, to try them that dwell upon the earth. I come quickly:
hold fast that which thou hast, that no one take thy crown. He that
overcometh, I will make him a pillar in the temple of my God, and
he shall go out thence no more: and I will write upon him the name
of my God, and the name of the city of my God, the new Jerusalem,
which cometh down out of heaven from my God, and mine own
new name. He that hath an ear, let him hear what the Spirit saith to
the Churches.

Rev. 3: 10–13

IN these days of terrible events many are seizing upon the
Book of Revelation in order, as they hope, to find there
information about the otherwise unknown *future*. They
have the feeling that we are fast approaching those days of final
crisis with which the Book of Revelation, like other books and
chapters of Holy Scripture, is concerned. They would like to
lift a little the curtain which conceals the future from us and to
know what is coming to pass. Is not the last book of the Bible
written for this very purpose? The Revelation of St. John the
Divine is a powerful work but also one that is strange and difficult to understand. It not only speaks of a book with seven seals
but it is itself such a book. Just think of all the prophecies which
have been deduced from this book and which yet have not come
to fulfilment—prophecies of judgment on other Churches or
sects and on the colossal figures of world history. In this sense it
is a dangerous book because it seems to nourish man's unhealthy
curiosity—that same curiosity which drives him to foretell or
to busy himself with horoscopes.

The Creator knows very well why He hides the future from

us and makes it impossible for us to know it in advance. Whoever wishes to overstep the limit which the Lord has ordained is attempting something which is contrary to the Will of the Creator. He is, as it were, assimilating the future to the past. The past can be surveyed. We can know it precisely, it is finished, consumed, so to speak, and hence we can gain a complete picture of it. It is as it were dead, however alive and present it may be in our memory. But it is forever unchangeable and irrevocable. What lies behind us is inevitably as it has been and not all our piety and wit can modify it at all. Were we to know the future in advance, that too would be just as unchangeable. In that case everything would necessarily have to come to pass as predetermined and we could neither add nor subtract one iota of it. The future as well as our own individual lives would also be a completed whole, unalterably fixed, just as in the calendar the eclipses of the sun and moon up to the year 2000 are already known because they can be calculated in advance to the very minute. Were the whole future thus preordained, then the freedom of decision and adventure would be excluded. Everything would have already been decided in advance. As in the case of our attitude to the past, it would only remain to us to look on at a scene which we could do nothing to change. Life would be a mechanical unwinding process. And it is just that which God does not will. He wills us to be and He has created us as men who are to decide for themselves and dare in uttermost freedom. Just because of that we are not to wish to know the future. The Book of Revelation has not been given to us to provide us with information about the future. Its purpose is rather to equip and strengthen us for times of testing and searching.

Holy Scripture does indeed tell us something about the future, viz. about the plan of God for the world and for ourselves. It tells us indeed something about the future course of events—but no more than we already know—that we must be watchful so as not to be surprised and crumple up like an army which has set no sentry posts or whose sentries have fallen asleep. Hence the ever-repeated warning: *watch and pray*.

It is in this way that we should understand this extract from the beginning of the Book of Revelation—the sixth of the messages to the Churches of Asia Minor.

It speaks about the hour of *temptation*—it would be better to say the hour of trial and the testing time which is to come upon the whole earth. The pictures of the future which we find in the prophetic writings of the Bible have this in common, that they speak of times of judgment, of times of severe testing, but not as does our own age in terms of progress. We men of the nineteenth and twentieth centuries have grown up with the illusion that the history of humanity displays continuous improvement. For this reason the outbreak of the first world war was such a shock. It did not at all fit into our view of the world understood to be getting better and better. And what has happened since the emergence of the totalitarian state and the second world war fitted even less into the picture. Men are so made that they project their wishes into the future. They suppose that the future must be according to their heart's desire—hence better than the present, more in accordance with peace, justice, and humanity. All this is of course understandable, but it makes the disillusionment so much the more painful. At the end of the war in 1945 I wrote in a Christmastide article that peace on earth, on which at that moment the hopes of so many were set, was not at all realizable in the immediate future and hardly to be expected. For this unforgivable pessimism protests rained down upon me and many of my own friends were very discontented with me. So great is the power of desire that it blinds us to the real state of affairs.

But the Bible is through and through realistic. It sees things as they are and never blurs our vision by a blue haze. It never tells us things are getting better and better but warns us in advance: terrible times are coming, times of trial which every one would like to avoid if possible. And the Johannine Revelation above all does not spare to paint these times of crisis in the darkest and most frighteningly gruesome colours—not to scare us but to make us prepared. If we know that evil times are coming we can be prepared beforehand. Just as we store food supplies for the times when our country, cut off from the outer world, will be in want, so also the soul can, so to speak, make emergency preparations for dark days ahead. For this reason alone the seer John or rather the Lord Himself speaks about what is to come.

He speaks of an hour of crisis and testing which is to come upon the whole earth. He means by that a time when it will be difficult to believe and dangerous to confess one's belief: when therefore there will be every temptation to lapse and deny one's faith or indeed to become a traitor and renegade. Many have already experienced times of this character: Christians in Germany under Hitler and even more Christians in Russia under communism. The fact is that just at present our memories are very short. We have already forgotten that in Russia several millions of men have already perished, many after frightful tortures, simply because they were Christians. We are here faced by a real and terrible persecution of Christians as in the time of Nero. Nor is this epoch past in Russia. Since the war there have arisen again and again waves of Christian persecution to which thousands fall victims. We had always supposed that this kind of thing happened only in antiquity. When I was young hardly any one thought that a time would again come when for the sake of religious belief a man could be tortured and killed as was the case with the martyrs in the days of the Roman empire. And now—at least from a distance—we have again experienced that very thing and are still experiencing it. Of course Russia is very remote from us and so we are not nearly so concerned about what is happening there as about the far milder type of persecution under Hitler in the Germany which is our neighbour. But most of us still live in the false security of supposing that such things cannot happen with us.

Friends, I do not wish to alarm you. That is not my duty. But I feel obliged to call your attention to the word of the Johannine Revelation about the hour of trial which is to come upon the whole earth. I do not say it will surely come very soon; but I feel it my duty to declare that it may well be imminent. No one can prove that it will not come. In recent decades we Swiss have been so wonderfully and mercifully spared that we have become accustomed to think no harm can touch us. The evil will halt at our borders. As though we had a right to immunity

73

among all the peoples of the earth, as though somewhere it were written—no harm can be allowed to touch Switzerland. We might indeed to some extent believe as much, were international agreements unchallengeable. Then our neutrality and therewith our security would be guaranteed. But we know of what worth such agreements are and how far a state which has made unscrupulousness its very principle of action will bother about our beautiful neutrality. Thus it is very possible—I do not say more but I do not say less—that quite shortly we shall experience a severe crisis of testing and trial just as much as Christians in Russia or Korea.

How shall we stand this test? The Church of Philadelphia receives a wonderfully comforting message: "Because you have endured and kept faith with me therefore I will preserve you in the hour of trial." Fidelity in return for fidelity. The Philadelphians proved themselves faithful, therefore the Lord wishes to be faithful to them. Is that message, my friends, addressed to us, to the Christian community of the town of Zürich, to the Christian churches of Switzerland? Because you have kept faith with me and have held fast to my word I wish to preserve you also?

Incidentally allow me to point out that the word preserve is equivalent to the Latin *conservare*, and that one who preserves or secures something may therefore be called a conservative. I only mention this point because many think to-day that conservatism necessarily implies something bad and retrogressive, for the simple reason that we are all smitten by the illusion of the idea of progress. But here at least the divine word plainly alludes to the idea of holding fast and preserving. Hold to what you have so that no one robs you of your crown. What is meant by this idea of holding fast? Is it something to do with saving or bank balances? Does it mean the maintenance of use and wont and traditional views? Certainly not. The meaning is clear from the context: the gospel of Jesus Christ, faith in Him, and the waiting for His coming.

Let me illustrate what I mean by reference to an experience which came to me recently. I was attending a conference of Christian workers from all countries, from Australia to Finland, from South Africa to Norway. Among those taking part there was a young Russian who as an officer of the Russian army was taken prisoner and for five years now has been doing Christian work among his fellow-prisoners. He was born and brought up in Communist Russia and was educated at communist schools and universities—as you know there are no others in Russia. His father, who was once a diplomat and later turned to the priesthood, was so persecuted by the communist authorities that his wife, the mother of the young man, collapsed and died from terror. It was his experience that one night his father was taken away and disappeared in the mines of Siberia. He has had no further news of him. He told me much about what is going on behind the iron curtain, about the persecution of Christians and their bravery. On one occasion—it was in the year 1940, hence shortly before Russia was attacked by Hitler's Germany—he was present at an Easter service in the region of Odessa. It took place in an isolated church, the only church in a vast area of hundreds of kilometres. But no less than 40,000 Christians came to this Eastertide celebration in order to worship at what was for them the greatest of all Christian festivals. The communists had organized a counterblast assembly and attempted to disturb the Christian worship in every possible way. Thus they later compelled these 40,000 people to listen to their godless communist propaganda for four hours. Then one of the Christians got up and announced his desire to speak. He was at first refused, but when he promised to say only four words they allowed him to come on to the platform. In unbroken tense silence the following words were heard: "Brothers and sisters, Christ is risen"—and the whole 40,000 responded with the Easter antiphon: "Yes, He is risen indeed." For 23 years amid bitter sorrows and dangers these men had safeguarded the word of Jesus and had held fast to what they had. It was a great comfort to me to learn that nearly half of the Russian people are still Christians after 30 years of godless propaganda and persecution, and that this percentage includes very many young people. My informant was himself an example and in him I became acquainted with a sincere and convincing Christian. Those men preserved and held fast the word of the gospel. They have stood the test. Would we endure with equal success?

Would we have the steadfastness to confess our faith in times of mortal danger? Would we refuse to deny it if by denial we could escape and by confession we might lose our life or our freedom, if the choice lay between the mines of Siberia and the denial of Christianity?

"*I come quickly*" says the Lord. But what does that mean? Already 1900 years have elapsed. How often have believers supposed that the end was now coming and it did not come! How many a time have the prophecies of Holy Scripture been used to calculate now this year, now that, with complete confidence and nothing happened; the course of world history went on its way. Hence many have come to the conclusion that it will continue to go on as a never-ending process without finality and with continuous amelioration. That in fact is the average opinion of contemporary humanity. But Scripture says otherwise. The historical process is moving towards an end and a decision. It is not for us to calculate when that will be. Nor can we picture to ourselves how it will come to pass. We know only two things. It will be preceded by a terrible time of sifting and testing and then finally the perfect Lordship of Jesus Christ will be realized. The time of persecution and trial and sifting may soon dawn. And then one thing above all will be required: the preservation of the faith intact and the proving of our loyalty in steadfast endurance. Everything will depend on this proving of ourselves, this unyielding steadfastness. On that will depend whether we receive the victor's crown and laurels or lose them eternally: whether we shall share in the ultimate victory of Jesus Christ or be separated from Him for ever. Not only does our present text confront us with the urgency of this decision but so does also the preaching of Jesus and of the apostles as a whole.

What can we do in order to prepare ourselves for abiding loyalty so that we may overcome and not be defeated? Much could be said on this point, and indeed all that we do as a Christian community is addressed to this end. But I will content myself here with singling out a few points of special importance. The first is that we should not fail to gather together on Sundays for divine worship and the hearing of the Word of God. But that is not sufficient. When the time of testing comes, as, for example, it has come everywhere in communistic countries, it is often no longer possible to hold regular services of worship. Churches in their thousands are being closed, priests and ministers killed or sent into exile. Thus it is necessary for us to be independent of the normal type of church worship and to find some means of hearing the Word as a result of which we need no longer rely on the public and official services. Of course it is said that we can read the Bible by ourselves in solitariness and that is true, thank God. Also we can and must pray alone in the privacy and silence of our chambers, as the Lord says. That too is true and important. But not in vain does the Lord say: "Where two or three are gathered together in my Name there am I in the midst of them." We must learn to read the Bible together and to pray together even without a minister or a church. Communion and fellowship in the hearing of the Word of God and in prayer is almost indispensable if the divine Word is to be a living reality to us. Most of us are unpractised in this, in fact we often feel averse to it. We suppose that all such things are trumpery and childish piety, unfit for the staid and sober Swiss. In the coming times of distress we might bitterly regret the fact that we have thought thus and have not taken care to furnish ourselves more adequately for those days when church doors will be closed and churches pulled down. And on the other hand, people who have already begun to practise this communal reading of the Bible and prayer have experienced the blessing which flows from it, and how often by this means the word of Scripture becomes so much more vital than when one reads it alone, and prayer so much more strengthening than the prayers of our solitude. Let us then not fail to seize the opportunities which our churches to-day offer us. Let us use them and practise this kind of fellowship. Let us practise the reading of the Word of God together in small groups and, as the apostle says, causing it to dwell richly among us.

In those parts of the world where Christians are persecuted it is not seldom the case that Bibles are no longer to be had. They are not printed, are not on sale; on the contrary, their circulation is forbidden. What is to be done in such circumstances?

One thing can never be forbidden: namely, what goes on in the depths of the heart. We may be forbidden to go to church, the Bible may be taken away from us, but the divine Word can never be torn out of our hearts. For this reason it is important to assimilate the word of Scripture so inwardly that we have a source of nourishment when outwardly the Bible is missing. Many of those who went through the suffering of concentration camp or imprisonment were deprived of their Bible but wrote out whole parts of it from memory for themselves or for others. Friends, how much would you be able to do under similar circumstances? How much could you repeat of the parables of the Lord, of the stories of the gospel, of the letters of the apostles, of the psalms and the prophets? The much criticized learning of the Bible by heart takes on at once quite another aspect and gains new importance in view of these times of trial.

A whole treasury of Christian theology and experience is preserved in our excellent hymn-books. You like to sing these hymns, you feel their power and the wealth of experience behind them. How much of them could you sing if you had no hymn-book? And one thing more—among many possible points—what a good thing it is when we are beset by personal difficulties and trials to discuss these hymns with a few friends, to note the Christian experience which they reflect and to take to heart their advice and the encouragement which they give us. How stupid we are not to make more use of such things! We bewail our weakness and yet neglect to tap this wonderful source of strength. I urge that we should now begin to practise these things according to the word of Scripture: "Work while it is day, for the night cometh wherein no man can work." Some time ago the government invited the people of Switzerland to store up food supplies against the time of need. Similarly I wish to advise you and all of us to store up spiritual supplies for times of trial.

Naturally, when we have done all this, it is not enough and in the last resort everything depends on one factor alone: that in our inmost hearts we should be faithful to God, that we should live in communion with Him, that we should love and trust in

Him and in the One whom He has given us as Mediator, Jesus Christ. To overcome means to cleave to Him when assailed by temptation and not to yield to the enemy, to cling to Him and not to doubt or despair.

And now in conclusion let us hear the *promise* which is given to all who endure and overcome. " Whosoever overcometh, I will make him a pillar in the temple of my God." That is a metaphor. The temple of God is the people of God in eternity when God shall be all in all. He who overcomes will enter the kingdom where there will be no more strife, no more doubt, no more assaults of temptation, where the victory will be won and the goal attained—the peace of God will reign and communion with God and His own will be triumphant. That is the ultimate reality of the future and this we know through God's word. But the decisive thing is not merely to know about it but to win through to it. Not every one will win—that is the solemn word of admonition which is spoken to us here as so often elsewhere. He alone will attain this final Presence who overcomes, who has remained true, who has held fast to the faith, and has thus proved himself in the time of temptation. A test is no test if in some way or another all pass it. A test is no test if it is not also a discrimination and a sifting. And that this ultimate test involves such a process is declared to us here with unmistakable clarity. Let us not deceive ourselves by any false comforts. It is nowhere promised in the Bible that all enter the kingdom somehow or other but, on the contrary, the promise is always made to those who prove themselves in endurance, who remain steadfast in keeping the faith.

So does everything depend upon us rather than upon the grace of God? That would be an entirely false supposition. For the meaning of abiding in loyalty to Jesus Christ and waiting upon Him is just that we trust solely in the grace of God rather than in ourselves. To overcome means to be unflinchingly certain of His grace even, and above all, when the power of evil seeks to persuade us that we have no part or lot therein and that we are lost. Jesus Christ came to call sinners to blessedness, not the righteous. We are admonished to be faithful to Him, the Saviour of sinners, the gracious God, to be certain of His grace whatever may happen; never to doubt that God is the unfathomably merciful One whatever terrible things may come to pass in the world. The climax of terror was reached when Jesus Christ the righteous was crucified. But precisely in that event God revealed the unfathomability of His grace.

The same thing is meant when the text goes on to add: "I will write upon him the name of my God and the name of the city of my God." Recall when the name of God was first inscribed upon you. It was in your baptism. Then the name of God your heavenly Father was as it were inscribed upon your brow. Hence we are sealed for the kingdom if only we remain true to this name. Then we know that we are members of this kingdom. And we know also that we shall have part in its eternal consummation. "Whosoever hath ears to hear let him hear what the Spirit saith to the Churches"—that means saith to *us*.

TWO KINDS OF SORROW

For though I made you sorry with my epistle, I do not regret it, though I did regret; for I see that that epistle made you sorry, though but for a season. Now I rejoice, not that ye were made sorry, but that ye were made sorry unto repentance: for ye were made sorry after a godly sort, that ye might suffer loss by us in nothing. For godly sorrow worketh repentance unto salvation, a repentance which bringeth no regret; but the sorrow of the world worketh death.

2 Cor. 7: 8–10

OUR text speaks about sorrow. The remarkable thing is that it speaks of sorrow as something positive, whereas we are all accustomed to think of sorrow in negative terms. In this respect all men are at one: they instinctively seek joy, happiness, good fortune, and avoid sorrow, just as they instinctively avoid death, illness, hunger and bad air, and instead desire life, health, fullness and fresh air. It is not otherwise in the Gospel and in the Bible as a whole. There life, happiness, joy and peace—personal fulfilment—are promised us, and it is taken for granted that every man would like to have those blessings and to avoid their opposite. Of course not all men seek joy, life and fulfilment in the same place and in the same way: but this does not alter the fact that they are all determined to seek joy and to elude the things that lead to disaster. Hence the words of the apostle in praise of sorrow seem to us unreasonable and even repulsive, contrary to nature and perverse. How can one speak thus?

But the apostle has in mind *two kinds of sorrow* which he sets in the sharpest conceivable contrast. The one kind of sorrow brings about salvation—hence fulfilment of life in the highest degree—the other kind of sorrow works death. Hence for him, too, as for all other men, it is in the last resort a question of the positive, of joy. It is to this end of course that he proclaims the Gospel, the glad tidings of great joy, of eternal life, blessedness and fulfilment, and it is in *this* context that we must understand his remarkable statements about sorrow. It is therefore a question of the healthy positive sort of sorrow which leads to salvation. And therefore the other type of sorrow is the morbid one, to be avoided, because it leads to death.

Strange as it seems to us at first sight, that the path to joy leads through sorrow, daily experience nevertheless affords all sorts of parallels to this state of affairs. In other spheres of life it happens from time to time, that one must do the exact opposite of what one really wants, in order to reach the desired goal. Whoever proposes to build a tall house must first of all burrow down into the depths of the earth; the taller the house is to be the more deeply must its foundations be laid. There is an old heathen proverb: *"per aspera ad alta"*—through the depths to the heights. This is something not quite unknown to the world. Men who have a deeper insight into reality than is common, realize that usually the way to our goal is not a direct route, but a devious one, and that supreme happiness and pure joy are not to be had so cheaply as the crowd imagines. The Latin proverb just quoted means: it costs something, it costs trouble and effort, sweat and tears, to reach the real heights of joy and exaltation. Life is not so cheap and easy to negotiate as we are apt to imagine and persuade ourselves. We have all experienced, of course, that the joys which are cheap lead repeatedly to disillusionment and the ache of emptiness. Our instinctive impulse to happiness precipitates itself upon what allures us with the promise of immediate and effortless joy and delight, and later we discover that, in yielding to the impulse, we have not really accomplished anything. The so-called night of joy ends with the morning of weariness and despair. Any one who has experience of the world knows that self-indulgence leads to satiety and disgust. In this point all the wiser minds of all ages are agreed: true joy is not to be had cheaply and easy delights are always followed by disillusionment.

This is the old and widespread wisdom of life. For this reason we can be certain that the apostle Paul means something different. For the Gospel is not simply one among the many more or less profound and proved truths of human wisdom. It is something which man cannot find out for himself by much reflection and by collecting and elaborating the insights which are the fruit of human experience. It is the revelation of God and hence far removed from all mere human wisdom.

In recent weeks, during Passiontide, Good Friday and Easter, we have again heard the gospel of divine self-revelation, the gospel of Jesus Christ, of eternal life, which the Saviour has disclosed and made accessible to mankind. The first chapters of the epistle from which our text is taken deal with this revelation of God in Jesus Christ, with the Cross, the Resurrection and eternal life. Once again we have heard that Jesus Christ died for our sins and to reconcile the world with God on the cross, that He rose again from the dead, and has thus brought us the certitude of resurrection and eternal life. We have too celebrated the Last Supper with each other; in brief, we have once again been ushered right into the great series of events which constitute the revelation of our salvation. And now the common round of everyday life has returned and the daily routine goes on its course with its cares and struggles, its ups and downs. What real difference has this message of Good Friday and Easter made, and how are we other as a result of this feast of the Lord's Supper? Perhaps we have once again heard the pregnant and inspiring words which occur in this same second epistle to the Corinthians, two chapters previous to that in which our text stands: "If any one is in Christ, he is *a new creature*; old things have passed away, and behold, all has become new." Is that really true? Or do we repeat it, simply because it stands in the Bible? Or does Paul think that we must believe this although objectively nothing is changed?

If so, the Christian community would not have conquered the world in so short a time. It would not have produced hundreds and thousands of martyrs, who were ready to sacrifice their lives for their faith. No, Paul really means what he says: if any one is in Christ, he has himself risen through the Resurrection to newness of life. He is speaking to such a community in his letter, to men who had really experienced this transformation of their being and had really been transplanted into this new and victorious way of life. The new creation was not merely an object of faith with them, it was a living experience which they described with such phrases as: life in the Holy Ghost, life in the power, the joy, the peace and the fellowship of the Spirit of God. We must bear all this in mind if we would rightly understand what the apostle says about healing sorrow.

Life in fellowship with Jesus Christ is not, therefore, as many pious people suppose and declare to others, a life of sheer joy, of unclouded heavenly radiance. To those very people who have just heard his message about the new creation in Christ, he now proclaims the truth about the sorrow that heals and saves. Hence he repudiates the idea of a Christianity which consists in uninterrupted radiant happiness. It is not in this sense that we are to understand his word about the new creation in Jesus Christ. Nor does he mean that we must indeed traverse the painful and shattering experience of conversion as a dark tunnel, and then once that is behind us we merge into the light and sunshine of the new life, and henceforth live day by day and hour by hour in the radiance of the new life which Jesus Christ has opened up to us, indeed, which He Himself is. Such a conception is not Biblical truth, but one of the illusions of religiosity. And this illusion, like every other, is inevitably followed by the bitterness of awakening to sober realities. Paul, like a true pastor of souls, wishes to spare us this painful process of disillusionment. In the very letter in which he has described so cogently the new creation in Christ, he speaks also about the healing power of genuine sorrow.

What does he mean by this? In order to make clear what it is and what it is not, he opposes it to the sorrow which leads to death, to the unavailing sorrow of despair. The former, the sorrow which saves, flows from God; the latter, which is vain and fruitless, springs from the outlook of the world. But how then can we distinguish the one from the other? The decisive and discriminating characteristic lies in the word: *penitence*. The sorrow of the world is always of such a sort that we grieve about outward circumstances which we encounter. Worldly fruitless sorrow is that which causes us to feel sorry for ourselves and to think: how badly things are going with me, how unjustly I am treated, how maliciously others behave towards me, how relentlessly unkind to me is fate. My friends, once our attention has been drawn to this, we realize what a monstrous part in human life self-pity plays. I would like to advise you to take a sheet of paper and a pencil in the next quiet hour that you have, and to note down at what points you too are guilty of succumbing to this vice of self-pity. Write as a heading on this sheet: The sorrow of the world which leads to death and despair.

But *true sorrow*, says Paul, is that which leads to penitence. Penitence is not something which we experience once for all in our so-called conversion. It is the same with penitence as with the clearing of weeds in the garden. The process must take place again and again as often as the weeds grow, for they cannot be rooted out once and for all. To be penitent means to recognize that the root of our troubles lies in ourselves. We all have our problems and our difficulties in life. Through penitence we must attain the recognition that it is I myself who am the real problem. You are in difficulties with your wife or your children or your colleagues or your chief. But it is their fault; who could not have difficulties with them! To be penitent means: once in a while to look at the reverse side and to discover what a difficult person *you* are, what your wife, your children, your colleagues or your chief must have had to tolerate from *you* and to what an extent you remain guilty in your conduct to them. To be penitent means therefore: to reverse the process for once and instead of blaming others, to blame oneself.

That is something which is completely contrary to our most ingrained tendencies. It is natural that we should not accuse ourselves but others. But faith, the supernatural life issuing in the miracle that God becomes real to us, begins with the fact that we do what is against our instincts by accusing ourselves. And that not merely in general terms. (As, for instance: "Yes, I know of course that I have my faults and that like all men I too am a sinner.") Such vague generalities are useless. They represent no real recognition, are not the fruit of any real penitence. The question and the challenge must be real and specific: what have my neighbours to put up with from me, how far am I guilty towards them? Then the heart-searching must go beyond that point or deeper than it, to grapple with the ultimate question. Only then comes the decisive challenge: how do I stand in the way of God, how is my dear ego an obstacle to the action of the loving God?

I must at this point make some reference to a small group of human beings, included in the scope of my discourse, yet in some sense forming an exception. I think that it is especially women who have a talent, in fact a quite obsessional tendency, to reproach themselves and to remain engulfed in melancholy. Must they also become penitent? Or is it that they are already too penitent? No, they too must repent of the fact that they remain absorbed in their feelings of wretchedness. Were they in the position of Lazarus to whom Jesus said: "Come forth, Lazarus, out of the tomb!" they would answer: "Thanks very much, but I cannot get out! I am already in the grave and there I intend to remain!"

Their guilt consists in the fact that they have, so to speak, wedded themselves to their misery and will not allow themselves to be released from it. Of course comparatively few people have this type of mentality. Most people are rather inclined to be quick in reproaching others for their misfortunes. Hence our inborn tendencies must be decisively reversed so that we enter into judgment with ourselves. That is the important thing and the great secret in dealing with our wretchedness.

What then have we gained by such sorrowful repentance and self-reproach—why does Paul describe it as a godly sorrow leading to *salvation*? With this question we touch the very centre of the Christian message. For what is the fundamental disease of the world and of humanity? Where lies the crux of the trouble in marriages which are not happy, in families which are disunited, in embittered relationships between employers and workers, between heads and their subordinates, and finally between nations? Is it not always reducible to one and the same thing: that every one accuses the other man instead of himself, has pity on himself rather than on others, that man with his beloved ego—I ought rather to say the pampered ego with which he is in love—blocks the action of the love of God? The "I" which stands in the way of God, the I which loves itself more than God and neighbour, the I which asserts itself at all costs—*that* constitutes the fundamental disease of mankind, the disease which the Bible calls sin.

Now, the mere fact that we enter into judgment with ourselves, rather than with others, does not effect the salvation of the world nor of ourselves. But when we do so, when we sit in judgment on ourselves, our eyes are unsealed to behold what God has done for us in Jesus Christ and what He wills to do in ourselves. We can never penetrate to the root of the matter; the root of sin is and remains for ever hidden from us. But Jesus Christ pierced to the root of sin and gave His life in order to tear it out and hence we can only participate in the benefits of the passion of Christ in so far as we—to use Paul's expression—allow ourselves to be crucified with Him, accept the judgment which God in the Cross of Christ has pronounced upon us, and concede the rightness of it. When that happens, then the corollary of it will happen too, that God for the sake of Christ accepts us as His own children.

But all this cannot come about theoretically or by means of a mere credal pronouncement. It can come about only in so far as we truly enter into judgment with ourselves. And that not once for all but repeatedly. Then the reorientation of our lives occurs.

Thus you can understand what Paul is getting at when he says: "Godly sorrow worketh repentance unto salvation which no man repenteth of." It is a matter of godly sorrow when you can accuse yourself instead of your neighbour: when you can realize that Jesus Christ died for you. At the same time you realize that you are then reconciled to God and are in fellowship with Him, and share in the new life.

At the conclusion of my discourse I return to the point I made at the beginning: when we build a house of several stories, we must first dig deep into the earth, and the taller the house is to be, the more deeply must we lay its foundations. We are now in a position to appreciate what is meant by this digging deeply: it is a question of godly sorrow which worketh repentance. Instead of having compassion on ourselves—"I think I have cause to be sorry for myself"—we shall want to begin to accuse ourselves before God and to beg for His forgiveness. When that happens, then a complete renewal and transformation of life comes about, the great miracle is accomplished that a man no longer trusts in himself but in God who forgives him his sins: that he no longer lives to boast of his own virtues, but to praise God for His mercy.

Such is the victory which springs from godly sorrow, leading to salvation through the penitence which we can never regret. Such sorrow is of quite a different character from the sorrow which flows from self-pity. For the latter type of sorrow has no issue. It agitates ever more and more within the circle of its problems and within the confines of our tragic wretchedness and despair. But the sorrow which brings forth the fruits of penitence has an issue: it leads through the cross of Jesus Christ to the resurrection–life of eternity.

Whoever digs into these depths can build securely to any heights, or rather: when we dig thus deeply, a tall structure is already raised. In so far as we yield ourselves in acceptance of Jesus Christ the Crucified, we already share the splendour of His eternal glory.

THE COVENANT OF GOD

(In commemoration of the entry of Zürich into the Swiss Confederation 600 years ago)

Behold, the days come, saith the Lord, that I will make a new covenant with the house of Israel, and with the house of Judah: not according to the covenant that I made with their fathers in the day that I took them by the hand to bring them out of the land of Egypt: which my covenant they brake, although I was an husband unto them, saith the Lord. But this is the covenant that I will make with the house of Israel after those days, saith the Lord; I will put my law in their inward parts, and in their heart will I write it; and I will be their God, and they shall be my people; and they shall teach no more every man his neighbour, and every man his brother, saying, Know the Lord: for they shall all know me, from the least of them unto the greatest of them, saith the Lord: for I will forgive their iniquity, and their sin will I remember no more.

Jer. 31: 31–34

THERE has been a lot of talk about our confederation in recent festival days and much that is significant has been said. It is a splendid thing, for which we may heartily thank God, when a people rejoices in the realization of its solidarity as a people, and when in particular it feels gratitude and pleasure for its polity which has grown up in the course of 600 years of history. There are not many nations which can rejoice in their political constitution to the same extent as we can legitimately do; for the peculiar feature of our cohesion and order as a state is just this, that it is a *federation*, a free commonwealth springing from mutual trust and goodwill. The people of Israel, too, in its early days before becoming a monarchy, was a similar federation or commonwealth. And so from the outset we may assume that the covenant which God concluded with the people of Israel through His prophets and His servant Moses, was not altogether without parallel to our own confederation.

But let us of course be on our guard against idealizing the covenant of our forefathers and reading into that historical event something more exalted than it really implied. That covenant was a mat ͞ of sober political calculation and states-manlike wisdom. It w ͜s admittedly sworn in the name of Al-mighty God, but yet it was not at all the same thing as the Bible narrates to us concerning the covenant of God with Israel, i.e. an act of divine revelation in which God Himself is the real initiatory partner. A wide gulf divides these two covenants, that of Moses and that of the old Swiss confederates. And yet there is a secret inner connexion between the two.

God had chosen His people of old on Sinai, that His Name might be glorified in them, but also that this people might be-come a free people. God chose as the form of His revelation the making of a covenant as though to say: I will indeed be your Lord, and you are to obey me, but I will not be your tyrant. Your obedience must be a free act, flowing from your own decision. This obedience towards me must make you free among yourselves. The element of reciprocity is always the decisive factor in a covenant. The compelling feature of the Old Testament revelation of God is that God the Lord enters with men into a relationship governed by reciprocity—i.e. a coven-antal relationship. But is it then possible, we may ask, that be-tween God and men there should exist anything in the nature of reciprocal relations? Can there be between two such unequal partners as God the Creator and man His creature such a part-nership as the character of a covenant presupposes? Now it is just this tremendous and astonishing thing which constitutes the revelation of God. God's relationship to His elect people is indeed that of the unconditioned, absolute Lord; but it is a relationship in which God by His word wills graciously to elicit the free response of man, and by His fidelity to call forth corresponding fidelity on the part of man. God does not treat man as an object with whom He can deal as He pleases, but as a subject, not as a thing but as a person with whom He speaks and whom He intends to speak to Him in return. That is the compelling fact: God puts between us and Himself His Word, through which He discloses Himself to us in such a way that we on our part may and must respond. This vital relationship of persons is the foundation of man's *responsibility*. In this way, as such a covenant partner, God wills to address man. Thus He endows him with both responsibility and *freedom*.

And now I would like to tell you something which few of you know because it is a bit of historical theology, and which, even among theologians, few know, because it belongs to the theology proper to Zürich. It can be no accident that it was pre-eminently in Zürich, in the Reformation theology of Ulrich Zwingli, that this thought of the Covenant was discovered anew, and made the centre of the whole structure of theological thought. It was those co-workers and successors of Zwingli, Leo Jud and Heinrich Bullinger, who drew the attention of Christendom to the fact that the grand theme of Biblical revelation, both in the Old and in the New Testaments, is the fact of the covenant which God makes with man. And from these Zürich thinkers, the idea spread into the whole theological world and exercised an important role in the understanding of the divine Word. I maintain it is hardly an accident that it was precisely the theologians of Zürich who made this discovery about the Bible: for as members of the Swiss confederation the thought of the covenant was so to speak in their very blood, whereas neither an Augustine who lived under the sway of the Roman emperor, nor Luther the subject of the Elector of Saxony, had ever so much as heard of a covenant. The Reformers of Zürich were above all free men as members of a free covenantal people, and hence they found it easier than others to grasp the mighty thought of God's covenant with man, and all that it implied about man's vocation to freedom.

Thus the Swiss confederation which we have been celebrating has its significance for the Reformation and the development of Reformed theology up to the present time. To-day it is again Swiss theologians who are placing the thought of God's covenant with man and the idea of human responsibility which it implies at the centre of their teaching. In doing so they are drawing not only on Holy Scripture but also upon the inheritance of their fathers which for them from the very start throws a flood of light upon the Biblical idea of the covenant.

The word of promise uttered by the prophet Jeremiah places in contrast *two* covenants. It refers to the old covenant which God made with the fathers, the Mosaic covenant, under the bitter qualification: that is the covenant which you have broken. That is an allusion to the covenant of Sinai which God made with His people when He brought them up out of Egypt, the house of bondage. This covenant was characterized especially by the law which God gave to His people. "They have broken my covenant and therefore I have rejected them" God says through the mouth of His prophet Jeremiah. They broke the covenant particularly in that they followed and served other gods, but also by heeding more the desires of their own hearts than the commands of God. When we hear that, are we not obliged to think at once of ourselves, we who so often pay more heed to our own caprices and wishes than to the will of God, we who repeatedly forge our own gods, our golden calves and other idols whom we serve while forgetting the true and living God? It is certain that the judgment of God upon us, the people of Zürich, cannot be less shattering than it was upon the people of Judah in the time of Jeremiah: you have broken the covenant and so I have rejected you. Unfortunately we Swiss suffer from a weakness which other people notice in us more readily than we ourselves: I mean self-righteousness, i.e. the opinion that we are without a doubt in the right, if only others were as much so as we. I am afraid that our present celebrations will have the subsidiary effect of confirming us in this attitude of self-righteousness. But, my friends, what we think of ourselves is not the point; it is what God thinks of us that matters. Are we not in danger of the judgment: you have broken My covenant and thus I have rejected you?

The god Mammon has turned your heart away from Me, the true God, and holds you in subjection so that we especially give people the impression that money rules the world and that the main business of life is to earn money and to acquire as much money as possible. Money is our national god, even though we do not say so openly and perhaps would not admit it to anyone.

And if it is not money, there are still many other idols who are worshipped in our houses and homes. We cannot escape the judgment of the prophetic word. Only let each one of us examine himself to discover what idols they are which are stealing his heart away from the worship of God and holding it under their spell.

But the marvel of the prophetic message is that Jeremiah is bidden declare, not only this word concerning the old covenant, the covenant which we have broken, and not only the judgment which follows as a natural consequence: "I have rejected you." He is commanded to speak of a new covenant, the reality of which lies in the future, a covenant of *reconciliation*, as a result of which "God will pardon your guilt and no more remember your sins." Jeremiah spoke these words roughly in the year 600 B.C.; and yet what he then declared was fulfilled 600 years later in the coming of Jesus Christ. The Lord speaks of this New Covenant on that last evening which He spends with His disciples in the eating of the Paschal Lamb. Breaking bread with them and handing them the cup, He says: This is the New Covenant for the remission of sins. The breaking of bread symbolizes for Him His imminent death on the Cross, when His body is broken; the outpoured wine is the blood which on the morrow will be shed. That is the New Covenant. Doubtless, in acting thus, the Lord had in mind the words of Jeremiah. The disciples, too, understood His words against that background, hardly so at the moment, only later on. Hence they came to view their fellowship in Christ as the fulfilment of Jeremiah's promise and themselves as the true people of God, the true Israel, the authentic heirs of the divine promises.

What then is the *difference* between the new and the old covenants? There must be a deep-seated difference; Jeremiah himself allows: not as the covenant which I made with your fathers, but something essentially different is this new covenant. Wherein precisely consists this difference? The first, the Mosaic, covenant, is based upon the law—but the law condemns us. Confronted by the law of God, we cannot stand upright, not even we respectable, law-abiding Swiss people. Were there nothing beyond the law which God gave through Moses, and which He has also written in the heart of mankind, then the last word to us also would be: I have rejected you, along with all that is beautiful and good among you in Switzerland. Let no festal joys deceive us on this point: in the presence of the divine law, we too, like all others, are sinners, criminals, "saboteurs", rebels, unrighteous. This truth must not be concealed even in a sermon preached in this festival season.

But now, by the grace of God, we are permitted to hear the message of this second, New, Covenant, which God has made with us through Jesus Christ and the essential nature of which consists in the fact that it is the covenant of reconciliation, of the forgiveness of sins, of the self-bestowing grace of God. Were this not so, did we not know as Christians that we live in the strength of this new Covenant, by faith in our Redeemer who has reconciled us with God by His death, I do not know how we could legitimately rejoice, once we had heard the word of the judgment of God according to the law. But we are of course a Christian community. We stand on the ground of the New Covenant, and through the Son may call God Our Father with all our hearts, and, as His children, invoke His Name.

There are many Swiss who do not do this and suppose that they can be good and right without such beliefs. But as for ourselves who believe in Jesus Christ and hold fast to His word of forgiveness and reconciliation, let us not sit in judgment on the blindness of these our contemporaries, let us rather believe on their behalf what they refuse to believe, and pray for them instead of condemning them. Let us seek in ourselves the responsibility for their unbelief as we reflect: have they had a chance of learning from us about the forgiving merciful goodness of Jesus Christ? Have we made them desirous, by the witness of our lives, of receiving what we have?

Assuredly it is sad, and must fill us again and again with apprehension and anxiety for the future of our people when we see how many of our contemporaries live without God, some even considering belief in God as outmoded and dispelled by our cultural enlightenment; and how they utterly fail to perceive that by this attitude they are undermining the foundations of a free state, and destroying the roots of a sense of responsibility, on which alone the well-being of our political and social order can rest. It is especially disquieting to see that so many of the leaders in science and culture, in industry and politics, seem to have understood nothing of the connexion between divine law and human law, between the sovereignty of God and the sense of human responsibility, between a free and truly human culture and the ordinances of God. But we who realize this should take all the more seriously our own faith, or rather the Word of God on which this faith rests, and remember our obligation to be witnesses of our Lord Jesus Christ—witnesses who, because they themselves live by the forgiving mercy of God, are also themselves merciful: who because they have experienced in abundant measure the goodness of God in Jesus Christ, reflect something of this divine goodness in their dealings with their fellow men.

Let us in this time, when we are thinking with thankfulness of the Swiss Confederation, remember so much the more that far more important covenant which God has made with us in Jesus Christ. The Swiss Confederation is an important part of world history and an important element in our earthly historical life. It must not be underestimated. But all world history passes away and we ourselves pass away. Nevertheless, when the hour strikes—and it will strike for each one of us and for some of us probably very soon—for us to take leave of this earthly world and to stand in the presence of God, then our Swiss passport will no longer be of any use and the certificate of our national status will have no value there. Then we shall be glad if we have another passport to hand, and can produce a certificate which will have validity in the beyond. Are *you* furnished with this passport and this certificate? It is noteworthy that in this heavenly passport stands not your name, but the name of Jesus Christ. He is the password. He is the Sponsor for our eternal home. You can and must refer to Him if you are not known in that country. That is what Jesus means by the New Covenant which He foreshadowed on that last evening and on the following day embodied and consummated. This fundamental gospel of the Covenant, signed with His blood, and sealed by His resurrection, is the sole means by which we can die comforted. But on it is written, not: for dying, but: for living. For faith in Jesus Christ makes us, not for the first time at death, but here in life, the beloved children of God. "Hence, whether we live or die, we belong to the Lord." Let us then live as His own, that we may also die as His own.

THE NOTES OF CHRISTIAN LIVING

Let the word of Christ dwell in you richly in all wisdom: teaching and admonishing one another with psalms and hymns and spiritual songs, singing with grace in your hearts unto God. And whatsoever ye do, in word or in deed, do all in the name of the Lord Jesus, giving thanks to God the Father through Him.

Col. 3: 16–17

IN these two verses the apostle Paul gives us an epitome of that in which the life of Christians consists and sums up the notes which distinguish it from the life of those who do not believe in Jesus Christ.

Is it really true then that there is something special about the Christian life? We must often have heard it said: you are not at all different from us pagans. Your churchgoing and your religious beliefs distinguish you only on Sunday morning from those of us who do not go to church and have no beliefs. What then does it all amount to? It is not worth the bother. You are no better as a result of it, hence it is not worth while.

Not only must we often hear such comments from others, but we often ask ourselves also, whether our discipleship to Jesus Christ really results in something plainly and strikingly distinctive, which could not arise apart from faith in Jesus Christ and in God. We must seriously put this question to ourselves. Of what value would be the whole apparatus of church life, preaching, church instruction, the order of church worship and all our almsgiving, if it produced no positive result? What would be the use of our more or less regular attendance at divine worship, if all in all our life were not fundamentally different from what it would be if we did not do all this?

In asking these questions and seeking to answer them, it will become clear that we are only beginners and bunglers in the

Christian life, and that our lives are not more different from those of other people only because we do not use sufficiently, and have not for a long time sufficiently used, what is given to us in faith. If the doctor gives us a medicine which we are to take three times a day, and instead of that we take it only once every other day, we must not be surprised if it does not properly take effect. In that case you have only yourself to blame; one must consistently take the remedy according to the prescription, otherwise it is no good at all. So it is with the medicine which is given us by our faith in Jesus Christ. If we do not use it properly then it is of no avail. Let us be clear on that point from the start.

And now let us see what the apostle Paul lays down as the principle of Christian living. He begins at once with the main point: *"Let the word of Christ dwell among you richly."* In the Christian life it is not a question of something which can take place as a result of our own efforts. We find in it no guidance for self-improvement. There are, of course, plenty of such directions from the cheap and trashy books which you can buy in the kiosk (*The Road to Success*) to the mystical lore of theosophy (*How to Attain Knowledge of Higher Worlds*). All these are attempts on the part of man through the exercise of his capacities and powers to bring forth something new and better. Such suggestions for improvement may be useful and right in this or that matter, but they are useless as regards the fundamental thing. For none of them goes to the root of the trouble. The trouble consists indeed just in the fact that men suppose that they themselves by their own powers, if only they had good intentions and used the right technique, could create a new and better world or make man into a new and better human being. To this the whole Bible gives but one answer: it is just that which you cannot do, nay, more, it is precisely the fact that you think you can do so which is the essential trouble.

But the Bible does not leave us with this answer alone. It does not say simply "no", it gives us God's "yes", God's action which really makes all things new, the unique and the all-embracing. It says: God has done this, God is doing it and God will do it. The name of this God who has done so, is doing so and will do so, is that of the Father who in His Son Jesus

Christ has had mercy on men and continues to have mercy on men, has helped men and continues to help men. This is He who was and is and is to come, the Saviour God who does what no man can do, and what is yet the one thing that must take place if humanity is to be changed. He reclaims us men who have gone astray from Him and so have come to grief and brings us back home to Himself. He restores the broken link between Himself the Creator and ourselves the creature. He Himself opens up the doors to the Father's house which we by our own trespasses have closed and closed in such wise that we cannot again open them; that is the Word of Jesus Christ, that is the Gospel, the great healing of the world and the universal atonement wrought by God, and as a result of which, what is missing at the root of our life because we have wantonly lost it, is restored to us, so that life becomes once again wholesome and whole. Such is the Word of Jesus Christ about the forgiveness of sins, and reconciliation with God which He has brought about by His coming, by His living and dying, by His cross and resurrection.

Let the Word of Christ dwell among you richly. This does not mean merely that we should go to church on Sunday. Certainly it means that also, for if we do not even do that, the word of Christ becomes alien to us. But something more is meant—namely, that the day must begin and end with this word, so as to be wholly embraced by it. Our Bible, or rather our New Testament, is like a spring from which we must repeatedly drink if our life is to be whole and well. Jesus once described Himself as the Bread of Life. But bread is useless if we do not eat it and eat it constantly. If we are undernourished, we are good for nothing. Many of us suffer from an acute undernourishment of the soul. What wonder is it that we are not able to show much fruit in those matters where Jesus Christ alone can restore and renew us?

Are you a prey to care and anxiety? No wonder, for care can only be dispelled when the soul is filled with faith in God from whose love nothing can separate us. Are you joyless? No wonder, for true joy comes into our lives only when that which is poisoning them is melted in the sun-like rays of divine love which destroys the deleterious bacillae in the soul. Are you loveless? Yes indeed, how could it be otherwise if you do not constantly replenish your meagre stores of love at the ever-flowing inexhaustible fountain of divine love, at that eternal spring called Jesus Christ?

Let the word of Christ dwell richly among you. We are still mere dabblers in this art. To our own soul's harm, we are again and again guilty of laziness. When you do not manure your field you must not be surprised if the grass is thin. If we do not nourish our souls, they will become just as miserably barren as a piece of land which you only want to exploit without putting anything into it. The proverb is apposite here: if we sow sparingly we shall also reap sparingly, if we sow richly we shall also harvest richly. Our soul is like a ploughed field and what makes it fruitful is the Word of God, the Word of Christ.

The second sentence of our text shows us still more plainly what miserable bunglers in Christian living we are. "*Teaching and admonishing one another in all wisdom.*" Here the apostle is referring to something which hardly exists among us: to the Christian fellowship in which Christians come together and help each other in the things concerning the life of faith and love. Consider, this is one of the fundamental weaknesses in present-day Christianity and one of the chief reasons for its lack of progress. The primitive Christian community was not at all a mere Sunday congregation, spending an hour a week in worship, listening to a sermon, praying a little, singing and then going off home again. It was a real brotherhood of which the individual members lived their whole life in fellowship one with the other rather than in solitary individualism. Hence it was possible to discuss all things with each other in the common fellowship, to advise and exhort each other. In such a community each placed at the disposal of the other the riches of his experience. Just think, a Christian life lived in individual solitariness, as is customary with us, must of necessity be a barren and wretched affair. It must be from the start a mutilated thing, an unreal thing, for Jesus Christ wished to put an end to just that —the solitariness of the individual religious man. In primitive Christianity we find so mighty a gale of the Holy Ghost, be-

cause the Church was a true brotherhood, because Christians
did not live in isolation from each other but in fellowship with
each other. Without that social element, the Christian life inevitably becomes stunted and starved, and has no chance of
becoming vigorous and creative. Thank God we are beginning
to understand this again and here and there things are happening which are calculated to rebuild such Christian fellowship.
Thank heaven the foolish opinion that all this is stuff and non-
sense is beginning to recede before the more informed view
that it constitutes the normal Christian life.

But the apostle refers also to something which accompanies
this fellowship. It must resound with *psalms and hymns and
spiritual songs*. In the Reformed Church, praise God, we have
retained that element. We have our own hymn-books and
anthem-books. But again we must ask why this singing should
be confined to Sunday morning. That was certainly not the
apostle's view. Perhaps some of you have been members of a
good church choir and have experienced how the singing of
inspired Reformation hymns has filled you with new life and
power. There is some mysterious quality about these hymns
and psalms which welled up from the heart, and are informed
with the power of the Spirit of God. Something of this divine
creative spirituality passes into us without our perceiving it
when we sing with all our hearts and not merely with our lips.
And since we are now on the eve of holiday time, let me say
from my own experience what a tonic it is to heart and faith to
sing such psalms and spiritual songs of the right sort, whether
alone or in company with others. Truly, one can sing oneself
thus into spiritual and mental health, one can sing oneself out of
darkling cares and harrying thoughts, and one can sing oneself
into communion with God. The apostle is thinking specifically
not only of formal worship but also of individuals in their
spontaneity: Sing to God in your hearts. We ought to practise
this a little. Perhaps at first it will be necessary to overcome
certain inhibitions, since the idea will strike us as somewhat
singular. I can only say: conquer your inhibitions. Take with
you on your holidays the new hymn-book with all those grand
hymns which it has restored to us. Take it with you in your

lonely walks and sing joyfully to the Lord in your hearts. You will see how the soul is enlivened and faith strengthened, indeed, what a heavenly blessing lightens the whole day by means of such singing.

But Paul is not referring to singing of any sort, he speaks of psalms and spiritual songs. What does he mean by that? Psalms are the prayers of the believing Church. A psalm is the human response to the Word of God. When we speak of prayer, we think far too exclusively of the petitionary element. But the psalms of the Old Testament teach us that praise precedes petition. To praise, worship, and honour God can only mean that with heart and mouth we echo what God has already spoken and done. When in the fellowship of divine service we praise and exalt the Name of God, our intention is to stir our hearts that our whole being may echo the voice and Word of God. His words ring out in the depths of our hearts, we try to reflect upon and affirm what He has already declared. We allow His word to penetrate and inform our mind, and to pierce the secret chambers of our hearts so that we assimilate it in our interior life. This exercise is of such great importance because otherwise we remain imprisoned in the circle of our own thoughts. And that is the exact opposite of what we mean when we speak of "living by faith". But when we praise and thank God, then our hearts are lifted up unto God and cease to be centred in themselves. By so doing we are occupied with the thoughts, the will and the goodness of God, and no longer with our own busy cares and schemes. Hence it is so important that we really do this and do it not only on Sunday morning but every day of the week. "Sing with grace in your hearts to the Lord"—by the singing of psalms and inspiring hymns let your disposition be moulded and penetrated by the Gospel message and by the praise of the omnipotence and mercy of God.

And now the final word: "*Everything that you do, in word or deed, do all in the name of the Lord Jesus.*" What we Christians must do in order to earn our daily bread is, of course, no different from what every one else does. But the point is not what we do but the disposition which we bring to bear upon our action. What the apostle expects of his Christian brothers in

Colossae is unheard of in the immensity of its significance: All that you do in word and deed, do in the name of the Lord Jesus. Is it not the fact that we fail at this point? None of us can say: yes, that is precisely what I do. Therefore I say we are dabblers and beginners in the art of Christian living. But we want at least to be beginners, and hence we must make a real start and should make continuous progress in this, that we live our lives not simply by revolving on our own axis, as all others do, but that we live them out as those who belong to Jesus Christ. This means that everything that we do we do as an act of worship, as those who know and remember that our life is not our own, but belongs to Him.

You will surely remember many affairs in which you have carried your point. "I had my own way." But, dear friends, a Christian can no longer have his own way, he must follow the way of Christ, his Head. The Christian life is one in which Christ, our Head, sways our life. In this regard, we must start all over again: we have not yet rightly understood this.

But now you are thinking it is a difficult and hard task to be always thus stretched in obedience to Christ. Hence the final message of Paul is: No, that is not so. The Christian life is a life of thanksgiving. I would like to ask you, I do not know you of course: do you really begin your daily work with thanksgiving or with a sigh and do you end it likewise with praise or in a cloud of gloom? Ah! my worries pursue me the whole night through. My dear friend, you are pronouncing your own judgment. Why are you harassed by your worries the whole night long? Why can you not put a stop to this constant flow of anxiety so that it ceases even to drip? Put an end to it, once and for all!

For this reason the apostle adds his final word: "*giving thanks to God the Father by Him.*" It is not a sour duty to stand and to abide in the service of the Lord, but a thing of joy which makes us cheerful and happy, because we are not merely servants whom the Lord commands, whether we will or not, but children and sons of God. We belong to His firm. He has made us partners in His business through Jesus Christ. God treats us not as aliens but as His own. It is not His profit which thus accrues, but our own. And this profit is put down to our credit. The note of thankfulness reminds us of this deepest mystery of the gospel, that God for our sakes has become man, that we might share in His eternal glory and His eternal life. He has released us from and wiped out the mortgage of debt which burdened our life, and has received us as partners, not because of our own accomplishments, but simply and solely because He loves us, and wills that we should enjoy the riches which He has. To live in this faith is therefore nothing but to live in the spirit of thankfulness that we are no more aliens who are coerced into the service of God but children of the Father who has given us His Son that thereby He might give us all things.

How far we are in earnest about the business of Christianity depends on whether we live in thankfulness and act and speak in the spirit of thankfulness, or whether we begin and end the day in care and sorrow: thus on whether our lives are motivated by the spirit of gratitude and inspired by joy because—praise and thank God—we can be no longer God's enemies, no longer mistrustful and unwilling servants, but may count ourselves as belonging to the household of God. Those who have put it to the test know what a difference it makes whether we begin the day with thankfulness or with care: and whether we end the day with praise or with sighing. But we have all done this in too small a measure so far. Let us make a new beginning in this spirit; let us no longer begin a day or end a day without thanking God. Then the bitter trials and sorrows which no one is spared will become transformed. It is the same as with swimming: so long as there is air in the lungs, we do not sink. So long as we cherish thankfulness to God in our hearts, the heavy load will not be able to drag us down. We remain on top, in spite of all our ups and downs. Hence let us be careful to see that air remains in our lungs, that gratitude does not melt away. And how could it vanish from the life of him who again and again occupies his attention with the word of Christ?

That, my friends, is the picture which the apostle Paul sketches of the life of the true Christian. It is a challenge to us to make a serious beginning with what he here prescribes as a task for us all. No one will regret making a start with it to-day.

IN NONE OTHER IS SALVATION

Then Peter, filled with the Holy Ghost, said unto them, Ye rulers of the people, and elders, if we this day are examined concerning a good deed done to an impotent man, by what means this man is made whole; Be it known unto you all, and to all the people of Israel, that in the name of Jesus Christ of Nazareth, whom ye crucified, whom God raised from the dead, even in Him doth this man stand here before you whole. He is the stone which was set at nought of you the builders, which was made the head of the corner. And in none other is there salvation: for neither is there any other name under heaven, that is given among men, wherein we must be saved.

Acts 4: 8–12

"IN none other is there salvation." When I think of or hear this compelling word of the apostle Peter I always recollect a conversation which I had two years ago in Madras, the capital of South India, with certain Hindu university professors who had asked me to explain to them how we Christians could affirm just this: "In none other is there salvation."

For it was precisely this contention which caused them most offence. The Indians are a religious people; as has often been observed, they are the most religious people in the history of the world. The word salvation or redemption is the focal point around which their thought has revolved from the most ancient times. Also in so far as they know Him, they have a great veneration for Jesus Christ. They like to include His name among those of the great bringers of light and healing to mankind. They disagree only at this one point—that He should be considered the sole source of salvation. I have seen on the banks of the Ganges a temple built by the Ramakrishna mission—to-day one of the most active of Hindu sects—where are displayed not only pictures of Ramakrishna and Buddha, but also of Moses,

Mohammed and Christ. All these names are honoured as those of founders of religions and bearers of salvation—Jesus Christ being one among them—and the learned priest-professor explained to us that men could reach the goal by many diverse paths. Each of these great names in the history of religion represents one of the ways by which—if they persist in it to the end —men can and even must arrive at the same goal which is the vision of the infinite One, of the all-pervading spirit who is the one true Reality. This point of view results in a tolerant acceptance of all religions, which—so it seems to Indians and to many Europeans of to-day—contrasts very favourably with the apparent intolerance and fanaticism expressed in the words of Peter: "In none other is there salvation."

This was implicit in the question asked by those Hindu professors of Madras. But I was glad that their frank question— Why do you Christians assert as much?—gave me the opportunity, without being importunate and impolite, of explaining what the apostle Peter means when he says—and why he says— "In none other is salvation, and no other name under heaven is given to men whereby they must be saved." For that in fact is *the* question to which the missionary in India and the preacher of the Gospel must give an answer to men of to-day, imbued as they are with the thought of tolerance. Why then this name alone? Why this intolerance towards all others?

Let me say a few words first of all about *tolerance*. The word may mean two quite different things: firstly, that we may not punish, persecute or harm any man because he cherishes and professes a different faith from our own, as was the case in former ages when heretics were burnt at the stake and dissentients simply wiped out. This sort of intolerance which unfortunately prevailed (for centuries) in the name of Jesus Christ is, thank God, forbidden to-day by the laws of the modern state and our insistence on freedom of religion and conscience. The state will no longer allow itself to be used by the Church as an instrument of such violent intolerance but on the contrary protects the freedom of every citizen, whatever his beliefs, from the fanaticism of all such as would wish to persecute him on religious grounds. We are glad and grateful that, at last, after ages of blind fury, religious persecution no longer obtains among us and that each man can practise and confess his faith, without having to fear harm and punishment from the civil authority or an all-powerful Church. In this sense we can only joyfully and without qualification affirm the thought of tolerance. To wish to use material violence in support of right belief is a terrible mistake which stands in sharpest contradiction to the New Testament.

But quite another thing is the Indian outlook which recognizes all religions to be in some sense true and so is able to venerate Christ alongside Rama, Krishna and Buddha as a parallel Saviour and Bearer of healing. This conception of tolerance has nothing to do with patience—for tolerance means patience—but requires the simultaneous recognition of the most diverse religious doctrines as true. Such a point of view—as those scholars in Madras rightly perceived—really stands in contrast to the Christian faith, as expounded by Peter: In none other is there salvation and no other name is given to us. . . . As Christians we must all affirm with Peter: In none other is there salvation. In this spiritual sense, we cannot be tolerant. Why is this?

First one might point out: this is so in all matters where it is a question of truth. The recognition of one truth excludes the possibility of recognizing its opposite to be true as well. Truth itself is intolerant. If it is true that twice two are four, then it is simply false to say that twice two are five or three. If it is true that Julius Cæsar was murdered on March 15 of the year 44 B.C., then it is just false to say that he died a natural death in the year 45. Truth is always single and exclusive. If there is only one God, then there is not more than one. The spiritually tolerant attitude of Indian religion implies secretly in fact the idea that none of the various religions is true in the full, serious, unconditional sense. Naturally we can admit very well alongside of each other any number of partial truths, so that we may say: That is true, partially, and the opposite is also true partially or up to a certain point. But if something is wholly and not merely partially, or to a limited extent, true, then this simultaneous recognition of something other as true is no longer possible; then we have an Either—Or.

But in my talk with my Hindu hosts I did not use this method of exposition. For in the last resort it could only have led to an argument as to who could lay claim to this possession of the whole truth: Jesus Christ or Rama or Krishna or Buddha and so on. I used quite a different mode of presentation which led us at once to the heart of the Biblical message concerning Jesus Christ. And here and now I would like to adopt the same method of argument. Certainly there is in all religions, and quite specially in the Indian religion or rather religions, the presence of a feeling of awe in the presence of the divine and the holy, something of the consciousness of surrender to this highest and holiest of which man is aware. That should not be disputed. And therefore we should respect and not despise any man who according to his lights is true to his own beliefs, however wrong-headed they may be. And we can grant even more to the Indian sages: it is true that you too are concerned about salvation and redemption, about what in the language of the Bible is called being saved or entering into life. Indians may rightly assert that much that is deep and true has been taught them by their saints about man's salvation. So much cannot be denied.

But one thing there is not in Indian religion or in any religion outside Christianity: a man who came on earth to reconcile to God by the sacrifice of His life those who had become separated from God by their guilt and sin. The Gospel of Jesus is just this —that we men are alienated from God by our sin and restored to Him by the fact that Jesus the Son of God gave His life for our sakes, as He Himself declared from the start: I came not to be ministered unto but to minister and to give my life a ransom for many.

I said to my Indian hosts—*you* speak of God, just as we do. *You* speak of the misery of earthly life, like ourselves. *You* speak of incarnations of the deity and of eternal life. *You* too have all these things. But one thing you have not: the One who died on the cross for the atonement of mankind and who from pure love gave His life a ransom for many. In this one point, you could not say: we have that too. Here, you would have to confess: that we have not got. Neither Buddha nor Krishna nor

Rama died for the sins of mankind: neither the one nor the other gave his life a ransom for many.

It now remains for me to make plain why precisely this is so important, so decisive, and why the apostle Paul in I Corinthians can say that his mission is to preach only one thing: Jesus Christ and Him crucified. At the heart of the Bible stands the idea of the *guilt of sin* separating man from God. This obstacle, this barrier, has been removed. We men feel and know many kinds of distress: illness, poverty, transiency, strife, hatred, war, death. We wish to be freed and saved from them all, for they are all very real distresses. But these sorrows do not constitute the central and fundamental evil. They affect, as for example illness and poverty, the outer circumstances of our lives. The essential evil is that which strikes you and me at the root of our lives as persons. That is the evil which flows from the fact that you are guilty in the presence of God. We may describe it as the personal evil. These other troubles do not hit me as a person, they concern the circumstances of my life. Although we men are not so acutely conscious of this fundamental evil—and in our own day, especially, ever fewer men seem to notice it—it is yet the real central and most important of all human evils. For here the point at issue is that we, in losing God, are losing ourselves.

And now the fact is that in no other religion, not even in the religions of India, is this evil understood in its full significance. Men crave for every possible kind of redemption rather than for redemption from *this* evil which strikes at the very heart of their being—from the guilt which burdens them. They have not appreciated the truth which the poet pregnantly sums up: the greatest of all evils is debt. Secondly, it becomes clear that other religions have not properly understood man as a *person*; for guilt, unlike other kinds of evil, is that which affects man in his personal being, the evil which affects not the concomitant circumstances of our lives, but ourselves, and ourselves at the core of our being, in our relationship with God. The guilt of sin means: all is not well between you and God, hence all is not well with you yourself: for the spiritual health of your being is dependent on your relationship to God. Your true life flows from your potential communion with God. If you are separated from Him, then evil gnaws at the roots of your life.

The Bible exposes and gives central significance to this most sinister of all evils—the fact that as a result of the guilt of sin we have become estranged from God. To this it says, and here is my third point: this evil can only be removed in so far as God Himself restores you to His fellowship by forgiving your sins. Herein is the essence of healing, and *true salvation*, that God reconciles to Himself and makes atonement for you who are separated from Him by sin.

It is just that which was effected through Jesus Christ and His atoning death. "He was wounded for our transgressions, he was bruised for our iniquities: the chastisement of our peace was upon him, and with his stripes we are healed." Thus runs the prophecy of Isaiah, and the prophecy found its exact fulfilment in Jesus Christ the Crucified. Through Him and in Him has God broken down the barrier raised by our guilt, and has once again linked us to Himself in peace and reconciliation, so that if we believe on Him the Atoner we are no longer estranged from God but at one with Him. The evil which corrupted our inmost souls is dispersed. We may again say to God: loving Father; and He replies: my beloved son in whom I am eternally well pleased.

That, my friends, is the gospel of Jesus Christ. Because that atoning event took place in Him and through Him alone—and not through Rama, Krishna, Buddha, or Mohammed—therefore He is the Saviour and His name the only name whereby we must be saved. Because already during the course of His earthly life Jesus forgave sins with full divine authority and held fellowship with sinners, the Jews rejected and crucified Him. But this very cross to which they brought Him in their blind fanaticism became the climax and the crown of His whole atoning work; for on the cross it became fully revealed that God's love is unconditional. "He who spared not His own Son, how should He not freely with Him give us all things?"

And so we may continue with the apostle and say: "For I am persuaded that neither life nor death, nor principalities nor powers, nor things present nor things to come, nor height, nor depth, nor any other creature, can separate us from the love of God which is in Jesus Christ." This unconditioned forgiving and atoning love is disclosed to us and bestowed upon us in Jesus Christ the crucified, and nowhere else, and thus He alone is our Saviour and His name alone is the Name whereby we must be saved.

GOD, OUR REFUGE

Lord, thou hast been our dwelling place in all generations. Before the mountains were brought forth, or ever thou hadst formed the earth and the world, even from everlasting to everlasting, thou art God. Thou turnest man to destruction; and sayest, Return, ye children of men. For a thousand years in thy sight are but as yesterday when it is past, and as a watch in the night.

Psalm 90: 1-4

THESE words of the Psalmist have no doubt been offered up as a prayer in many homes on New Year's Eve or New Year's Day. Hence it is very fitting that to-day, when we have just recently entered on the New Year, we should hear their compelling message and try to understand the truth that God wishes to convey to us through them. "*Lord, Thou. . . .*" Here speaks a man, a frail and transient creature, well aware of his frailty and transience, with God his Creator. This psalm, like all the psalms, is a prayer. But this very prayer suggests to us in a peculiarly striking fashion what an extraordinary thing it is that we are able to address Him, the Eternal and the Infinite, in these terms: Thou, Lord.

Every time I pray I must repeatedly thank God because I can and may address Him in these words: Thou, Lord. For, must we not agree, this is not at all a self-explanatory state of affairs. How many men to-day are not able to do this. They cannot call, out of the deeps of the transitory, death-shadowed world, out of the confusion and nothingness of their life: Thou, Lord. They do not know what such things are about. They are self-enclosed and solitary, alone with their anxieties and fears, alone on the way—ah! how short!—in which death is ever drawing nearer to them, nearer and nearer each day with no possibility of escape. Death is coming to me and I must needs go to meet it as in a yawning abyss which swallows me up. Such men have only this one dimension, their journey on this earth, which death must terminate. They are not aware of the third, the vertical dimension, as a result of which we can invoke the Lord: Thou, Lord, Thou eternal God. Where this third dimension is lacking, life is merely a plane surface without height or depth and becomes in the literal sense of the word "superficial". However cultured and intellectually interesting such people may be, their life is crushed and flattened to a mere superficies, without depth or height. It resolves itself into a path on which one is ineluctably confronted with death and annihilation. And therefore their life has no meaning. If death, destruction, is the end, then life is just meaningless. If the vertical dimension, the heights and the depths, are lacking, then life is confined to the horizontal plane of earth and as such is meaningless. And because it is meaningless it is ultimately engulfed by despair. It is really no accident that at a time when so many men have ceased to be able to pray, the theme of despair, meaninglessness, nihilism, stands so prominently in the foreground and meets us everywhere, in the books that we read, the plays and the films that we see. It cannot be otherwise. If the third dimension is lacking, if we cannot call upon the Lord, the Eternal, then there remains only senselessness, despair, nihilism.

But the very moment when I can pray and my heart can call out: "Thou, Lord," despair vanishes, the vertical dimension is restored, eternity is present with us. Death is not the final word, life is no longer a journey confined by the earth's surface, ever advancing towards death, beyond which there is nothing. Then some other factor is present, not inexorably limited by death, but something which transcends death, which exists eternally, God who summons me and to whom I respond, eternity which I go to meet and which comes to meet me. Thus life ceases to be meaningless and despairing. It has assumed a meaning, an eternal meaning. "*Lord, Thou hast been our dwelling place in all generations.*" The man who prays thus—we do not know his name any more than we know the names of the writers of other psalms—does not pray alone. He knows that many pray with him and many have prayed before him, he stands in a real communion—perhaps at the moment an invisible communion—with all those who have prayed with him and are still praying, whose prayer soars upward like his own, and in community with whom he knows therefore that he is engaged in a pilgrimage—the goal of which is encounter with the God who is ever seeking him and all who thus pray. This community of those who pray is called in the Bible, church, ecclesia, people of God.

Thou hast been our refuge from one generation to another. It is not the speciality of pious or religious men that they seek their *refuge* in God, whereas other men seek refuge elsewhere. The truth is that there is no other refuge but God, so that those who cannot believe and pray are simply without refuge. Refuge means the unshakeable ground beyond the ever-flowing stream of time. Refuge is, as it were, the accessible island in the waters of the world's life which devour all. There alone is one securely anchored, there alone can we plant our feet on firm ground, in the land of eternity encircling the earth which is ever flooded by the waters of death. There is no other unassailable ground, for all other points of refuge are themselves part of the onward rush of the time stream. All else belongs to the surface, to the horizontal, to which one is confined without hope of rescue until the moment when one becomes sensitive to the presence of God and can address Him: "Thou, Lord."

This refuge is the sphere of peace. Men who have found refuge because they have found God, are men in whom reigns the peace of eternity. However much they may be harassed and vexed and burdened by all sorts of cares, yet in the last resort they are men who know the secret of transcendent peace, because they have their feet planted on firm ground—the ground of eternity. They have a standing ground. Whoever can call upon God and pray to Him stands unassailably amidst the sweep and eddy of the time-stream and the mighty convulsions of world history. Hence we meet constantly in the Bible the metaphor describing God as our rock and our shield. He who can invoke God is one who has built his house upon the rock. He is in touch with something which abides, to which the revolutions of time and the world wars and the collapses of history can do no harm. In God there is security, provided we are really in God, really standing on the ground of eternity.

Modern men long for security. This is why insurance companies are so prosperous, why the totalitarian state and communism which offer security to men have such a power of attraction and why so many to-day are going over to the Roman Catholic Church. Security! But there are pretended securities which are illusory because they do not tower beyond the flow of time into the realm of eternity, because after all they are only constructions of human power. "What men have built, men can destroy" it says in *Tell*, and the whole of human history is one single extended proof of the truth of this saying. The towers of Babel which men rear proudly to the skies collapse sooner or later with a thundering crash: the thousand-year empires break up even before two decades have passed. All this tumult belongs to the horizontal plane of this world, from which depth and the vertical dimension is lacking, for that is to be found in God alone. He alone offers real security, for He alone is from everlasting to everlasting.

We speak of the eternal hills or of the eternal thunder of the ocean. But that is an exaggeration. None of our mountains is eternal. Our geologists can tell us of each one, with a fair degree of accuracy and certainty how old it is—so many thousand or millions of years. Not even the earth is everlasting; that too came into existence at some specific date, so many—perhaps four million—years ago. God alone has no beginning; He exists eternally, transcending whatever has a beginning. God is the Creator of all things. Our thought cannot grasp this conception, however familiar the word Creator may be to us. We simply cannot imagine how God created the world out of nothing. Of course we find in the first chapter of the book of Genesis a so-called account of creation. But the object of this is not to tell us how the process occurred, one thing being created after another. The intention is to impress upon us this one truth: everything which belongs to our world was created by God and that effortlessly, without any special activity, as is suggested in Psalm 33: "He spake and it was done, He commanded and it stood fast."

Many have supposed that this Genesis story of creation stands in contradiction to modern scientific knowledge. That is a complete mistake; for the two accounts deal with quite different things. The creation story declares that everything, heaven and earth, plants and animals, originated through the creative "fiat" of God. But the natural sciences explain to us how one thing has evolved from another in the order of temporal succession. The Bible tells you: you live in a world which God created, and you yourself are part of this divinely created process. But God stands before, beyond and above all that. He is your sovereign Lord, for He is from everlasting to everlasting.

Because God, He alone, exists beyond all that has come into being, therefore He transcends the flow of time like a rock in the midst of a rushing river, unmoved, eternally the same, unshaken and unshakeable. Hence only He can be our refuge. Everything else passes away and we pass away too, if we are not saved from being engulfed in the onward sweep of time by coming into living contact with the eternal God. Thus to encounter God is the work of faith: but the lifebreath of faith, from first to last, is prayer—the kind of prayer in which we address God thus: Thou, Lord, art our Refuge. By this faith, this calling upon God in the life of prayer, we step out of the rushing waters of time on to the firm ground of eternity. Well for him who does this and to whom it is granted to do it. Well for him who does so when he hears God's voice: I am He who has created you and named you, therefore you can call upon Me.

Have you noticed that the Psalmist does not say: "Before the mountains and the world were made, Thou *wast*", but "Thou *art* God, from everlasting to everlasting"? He means by this: the being of God transcends the forms of time, it has neither past nor future, it is eternal Present. Perhaps you recollect that in the Revelation of St. John we find the words: "He who was, and is, and is to come." To be correct, this is an allusion to Jesus Christ, the Revealer of God, who comes to us from eternity into time in order to draw us from our transient and fleeting mode of being into the plenitude of eternity. But here in the Psalm the subject is God as He is in Himself. He transcends all the spans of time: He is eternal Presence. For Him nothing that is past is past; nothing that is future is future. As He is omni-present and all-encompassing, so everything is always present to Him. His eyes saw you when as yet you were not, and His eyes see you as you will be when you are dead. Hence there is no forgetfulness in God as likewise there is no remembrance: both past and future are present to Him in the eternal "Now".

Hence for God there are no divisions and measurements of time. A thousand years are but as yesterday when it is past, i.e. a mere nothing. *We* are conscious of time as measurable. Many a time-period seems to us painfully long, ah! too long, and many a one seems all too short, ah! but a fleeting moment. How agonizingly long the night drags on for the sick man tossing in pain in the hospital. How short the meeting between two human beings who love each other, and have not seen each other for years and to-morrow must part again—how swiftly gone are those few hours of reunion! How long does a nation feel a period of twenty years' subjugation to a foreign power which causes it suffering: how short a century or two centuries spanning a flowering period of human culture like that of ancient Athens or that of the Renaissance! How diverse and relative are our impressions of periods of time! But for God such measurements of time do not exist. Even a thousand years are for Him but as yesterday when it is gone, even a million years but a fleeting moment.

Of what use can it be to us to make this clear to ourselves? Still the night of pain drags out its weary length for us, and the day of happiness vanishes. Certainly: but if you pray when you are in sorrow, if you in faith lift up your heart to the eternal and ever-living God, a change comes over your experience of pain, as also your experience of fleeting joys is transformed. A ray of eternal peace and blessedness steals into your night of bitter sorrow and weeping: the light of eternal holiness imparts new meaning to your brief day of happiness. You are no longer simply the victim of the human consciousness of time. You are freely given a secret participation in the eternity of God. You know then that your pain will ultimately be dissolved in the eternal blessedness of God. You realize then that your earthly happiness is not the final end and meaning of your life.

Lord, Thou hast been our refuge from one generation to another. We are somewhat surprised to note that the same man who says that, continues: "*Thou turnest man to destruction, and sayest: Return, ye children of men.*" Is death then the ultimate reality? If so, how can God be our refuge? Here, it is relevant to observe that we are in the twilight dispensation of the Old Testament, in the period when God has vouchsafed part but not the whole of His revelation. He has revealed of course His omnipotence, His wisdom, His righteousness; but not yet the fullness of His love, in its counsel and operation. That happens only in the New Testament, in Jesus Christ. In the eternal radiance of Christ, we may thus understand the words, "Return, ye children of men": I, your heavenly Father, who have created you—you who have succumbed to sin, death and sorrow—I call you forth out of your wretchedness and restore you to My eternity where sin, death and sorrow are no more. Hence only in Jesus Christ can we without hesitation or qualification say to God: "Lord, Thou art our refuge."

No doubt the Psalmists already knew something of the grace of God who forgives us our sins and redeems us from corruption. "Praise the Lord, O my soul, and forget not all His benefits. For He forgiveth thy sins and healeth all thy diseases." Thus Psalm 103. But the Word has not yet become flesh; the Saviour has not yet been born; the redemptive plan of God has not yet been fully disclosed. For only through Him, Jesus, the Saviour, do we know that God does not remain aloof from us in His eternity. He comes to us clothed in temporality in order to bestow upon us eternity. He the eternal God has become man in order to invest us creatures of time with eternity. Hence we do not advance inexorably and irredeemably towards death, as they suppose who do not know God. It is our faith that "Whosoever believeth on Me will live though he die."

For this reason we need not have any serious fear about anything which may happen to us in this world of time. We do not know what the New Year may bring. But bring what it may, one thing we know: we are moving not towards death but towards eternal life.

THE MEANING OF THE LAST SUPPER

The cup of blessing which we bless, is it not a communion of the blood of Christ? The bread which we break, is it not a communion of the body of Christ? seeing that we, who are many, are one bread, one body: for we all partake of the one bread.

1 Cor. 10: 16–17

WE have in the New Testament four different accounts of the meal which the Lord shared with His disciples on the eve of His crucifixion and which, in remembrance of His death, we celebrate as the sacrament of the Last Supper. These four accounts, which we find in Matthew, Mark, Luke and Paul, all differ somewhat from each other. The oldest of them is that of Paul, which is to be found in the eleventh chapter of 1 Corinthians. It was written no more than twenty years after the event itself, thus at a time when most of the disciples were still alive. Since that date, the cult and the doctrine of this rite have undergone a long and complex development, and around them has been woven a real passion story. The sacrament which was to have united Christians has become an apple of discord, rending Christendom up to the present day, and even setting by the ears our own reformers Luther and Zwingli. Hence it becomes necessary for us to ponder anew the meaning of that mysterious rite of the Church, which from ancient times has been described as a sacrament.

For many centuries the opinion has prevailed that in this rite a marvellous transmutation takes place in the two elements of bread and wine. One might almost say: something magical, in that as a result of the utterance of the priest who speaks the words of institution, the bread becomes the Body, the wine the Blood of Christ. This interpretation has always been specifically based on the words of our text from 1 Corinthians. For do not these words suggest precisely what is expressed in this doctrine of *transubstantiation*? If this were so, then in the divine service of the Eucharist we should be faced by a sort of magic. Christians would be provided with a sort of magical food— namely, the Body and Blood of Christ. And that is of course what the Roman Catholic Mass means and claims to operate. In catholicism it is further asserted of this magical food, that it is a means of attaining eternal life, according to the expression of an ancient father of the Church: "a medicine of immortality". It is easily understandable how as a result of its control of this divinely-magical technique the priesthood assumes a powerful significance: it can dispense and refuse eternal life. The Christian Church thus becomes an institution for the dispensation by magical means of healing and salvation where, by the pronouncement of the priest, the bread and wine are transformed into the Body and Blood of the heavenly Lord and are distributed by him as a medicine of immortality.

But to any one who studies the life and teaching of Jesus in an unprejudiced way, this whole magical approach must appear in rather an incongruous light. If we read the writings of the apostles we find not the slightest trace of such conceptions. In the total corpus of Christian doctrine as based on the New Testament, a Eucharist of this kind would stand out as an irrational surd. But again and again it is this element of magic and mystery which attracts men with a secret and compelling force, and which meets their need for the tangible manifestation of the divine, for a visible marvel and an embodied salvation. It is here rather than elsewhere, that the mysterious power of the priestly Roman Catholic Church is rooted.

But what then did the apostle mean when he uttered these words? For he too is thinking of a real objective mystery, a *miracle* which takes place when in the Church of Jesus the holy meal is celebrated. Hs is not thinking merely of a memorial feast. A purely symbolical representation of the Last Supper of Jesus and of the significance of His death on the cross is not a miracle, but at the most something poetic and artistic. The apostle is not really concerned about such things. We understand best what he means if we place his interpretation of the

Last Supper in the whole context of the apostolic message. The point is just that we should interpret his Eucharistic doctrine in such wise that it does not appear as a foreign body in his Christian doctrine as a whole, but is intelligibly adaptable to the latter.

The apostle constantly preached Jesus Christ as the Saviour of mankind. In Him God drew near to us men. We men are in fact living in alienation from God. Our life moves on a plane that is very remote from God—not spatially remote, for what could that mean in face of the omnipresence of God—but remote in an inward and spiritual sense. We live as though God did not exist, we live without recollecting the presence of God, as though we were alone and the masters of our own lives. That is our empirical condition. Thus men live by their own sole resources, thus we all live until God steps into our lives, until God makes His presence felt within us and becomes our ruler and guide. Life without God—that is what Paul means by sin. And the fact that God Himself enters our lives, claiming recognition, is what he means by revelation. This revelation is mediated through Jesus Christ. Of course apart from Jesus Christ we have our own views of the divine: even apart from Jesus Christ we are not simply atheists. We cherish perhaps our own philosophical or religious world-view of which the corner-stone is something such as a first principle which we call God. We have also our private ethical systems. We recognize the law of conscience, the moral law. All this the apostle does not deny. But, he says, it does not alter the fact that you live your own lives as though you were your own masters. God is only an idea of yours, a point in your system of thought. *You* give to God the place which you think appropriate. *You* are the masters. But now it has happened that by the sending of His Son Jesus Christ, *God Himself* draws near to you, discloses Himself to you and bestows His life upon you, making Himself Lord in your lives. But not a Lord according to your conceptions of lordship and not as you yourselves wish to govern and rule. God made Himself Lord by becoming a servant, by washing His disciples' feet, by being obedient unto death, even unto the death of the cross, in such wise that He the righteous and the sinless one loaded Himself with the curse of sin for your sakes, for you—unrighteous and sinful men—that you might no longer be crushed by the power of sin. Whoever believes in this crucified Lord, whoever accepts the action of God by which He takes this condescending way in order to meet and find us who live so far below Him, whoever says to himself: you live at an infinite distance from God and are infinitely inferior to Him and God Himself must enter this inferior and alienated world in order to encounter you, He Himself must penetrate to the heart of the curse and punishment in order that you might go free—when, I say, you are persuaded of that, then God in Jesus Christ becomes the Lord of your life. Then the death of Jesus Christ, from being a catastrophe, becomes the victory of God over you and your godlessness, then He draws you into His own eternal life, enabling you to share in His resurrection and making you by this means a new creation.

Such is the gospel which the apostle Paul—and the other apostles with him—proclaimed. It is *in this context of thought* that we must attempt to understand the rite of the Last Supper which Jesus celebrated with His disciples and which they, obediently to His injunction, "This do in remembrance of me", re-enacted regularly on the first day of the week in face of the assembled Church.

Why did Jesus command the observation of this rite? He did not give His disciples any other similar instructions about divine worship. Why this? Is it not sufficient to preach and believe His gospel, the gospel of His atoning death? Why this ceremony in our churches? For a long time I asked myself this question—as no doubt many of you have done—without finding the right answer, until the answer sprang to my mind from this text: we must note the dual meaning of the phrase *"Body of Christ"*. On the one hand it refers to the body broken for us on the cross at Golgotha: this is symbolized or figuratively expressed in the broken bread, just as the outpoured wine represents the blood of Christ outpoured for us on the cross. That is the usual interpretation which we are familiar with from our Confirmation instruction. It is correct in so far as it goes, but it is incomplete. For the Body of Christ means in the New Testament something else: the Church. The latter is the Body of Christ because Christians are incorporated into the eternal Christ by faith and the Holy Ghost. Thus our text says: We who are many, are *one* body. There arises from us who are a multiplicity of individuals, a unity, something whole and cohesive, kneaded together.

Thus what is effected through the common participation in the atoning death of Jesus Christ is the unity of the Church. This is objectively brought about by the fact that the Church community eats the bread and drinks the wine in fellowship and in doing so shares in the atonement wrought by the death of Jesus, in the body broken for them and the blood outpoured for them. Here is no magic, the bread is not transformed into the Body, nor the wine into the Blood. But a miracle *does* take place in that those men who formerly were their own lord and master, now are ruled by the one Lord, and so from a manifold of separate individuals, each living and caring for himself, there arises a unity, one body, of which each believer is a member and Jesus Christ the Head, controlling and guiding all. In the eating of the bread and the drinking of the wine, Jesus Christ Himself is present to them all and constitutes them as a unity which He controls and directs. They become the Body of Jesus Christ.

Such was the experience of the disciples: in that, obediently to His injunction, they ate the bread and drank the wine, they experienced His living presence in them and amongst them, making them miraculously a unity incomprehensible to themselves. I say: Here we have a *miracle*, but *no magic*. Magic means the transmutation of the bread and wine by the utterance of the priest: but miracle is the presence of Jesus Christ, making His own into a unity, into one body. Thus the sacrament of the Last Supper is truly a miraculous event but not a magical event. The miracle consists in the creation of a believing community of which Jesus Christ Himself is the indwelling Spirit and Guide.

So long as we do not accept Jesus Christ in faith, we are, as I said, our own masters and so recurrently in disharmony with each other. Each conducts the business of his life as he thinks fit, and in competition with his neighbour. But when Jesus takes possession of our lives, this self-will ceases, and is replaced by obedience and fellowship. Thus faith implies community without qualification. One cannot be an individualistic Christian. To become a Christian means precisely this, that one ceases to be an individualist, a man living on his own lines. Living for oneself alone comes to an end when Christ enters into human life. In place of individualistic living, arises brotherly concord which impels us to live for others. Is then the Last Supper only a symbol, a pictorial representation? It is a symbol, but it is *not merely* a symbol, it is also an objective reality, a miracle. When it is partaken of in faith, when the bread and the wine are so received that each communicant shares in the death of the Lord and experiences the effectual reality of God's atoning action, then something objectively real takes place. Then there occurs in fact a transformation, but not a transformation of a substance, bread, but a *transformation of human personality*. From self-willed individuals, living in isolation from each other, they become members of the Body of Christ, no longer their own masters and thus no longer living for themselves, but controlled by their Lord Jesus Christ and hence living for each other.

My friends, is all this true or are we imagining things? Does a real miracle here take place or do we only act as if. . . .? It is at any rate quite clear that the primitive Church experienced the actuality of this miracle, and that the apostle could speak of it to all because all knew: that is certainly true, we have thus experienced the miracle and experience it ever afresh, as often as we celebrate the meal in fellowship. But it is equally clear that *we* do not have this experience as a rule when we partake of this sacrament. No miracle happens, we feel the impact of no new reality, it is a mere ceremony in which we co-operate, because that is the custom, and especially because it is thus prescribed in the New Testament. I say: as a rule. The other, the uplifting experience, occurs at times, as suggested in the New Testament and as was experienced by the primitive Church.

Whence then arises this difference? The answer can be given in two words: *faith* and *Christian fellowship*. And both imply the same thing: for where genuine faith is, there is the spirit of community, and where community is, there is faith. But then of course neither faith nor community mean what we normally understand by those terms. Faith cannot be reduced to the argument: that is what the parson says, what the catechism says, what the Bible says, and therefore I take it as true: that attitude is at most a preparation for faith. And the fellowship of the Church does not mean: since we all confess the name of Jesus Christ, therefore we form together a Christian community: that again is at most only a preparation for real fellowship. Faith means rather: you sincerely recognize that you encounter God in Jesus Christ, that in Him God addresses you, slays your masterful self and becomes Himself your living Lord; and Church fellowship means: we, who formerly meant nothing to each other, are now brothers and sisters in Christ. There flows through and animates and controls us, *one* Spirit, the Spirit of the Lord.

When that reality is effectually present in the celebration of the Eucharist, then of course occurs the miracle of transubstantiation. And when this miracle takes place then the fellowship and unity of the Church becomes real. This kind of transformation, this growing into a real community or body—that is the fundamental issue in Christian faith. This process forms an answer to the questing of men to-day for truth and for community. The answer runs: Christ is the truth and in Christ is community. So-called existentialism seeks the truth which emerges from the crises of living. So-called communism thinks that it possesses the truth which creates communal life. But neither does the former lead to the discovery of truth, nor does the latter lead to the realization of fellowship. These things can only happen when God in Jesus Christ becomes a reality to us and so transforms us that we are at one with each other. The Last Supper, truly understood and experienced in its truth, i.e. as "communio", is the real answer to the questions of our time. May it please God that what we have now recognized as the truth in fellowship with each other, may take shape and substance in our lives.

DEATH AND RESURRECTION

Blessed be the God and Father of our Lord Jesus Christ, who according to His great mercy begat us again unto a living hope by the resurrection of Jesus Christ from the dead, unto an inheritance incorruptible, and undefiled, and that fadeth not away, reserved in heaven for you.

1 Peter 1: 3–4

PERHAPS you are surprised that to-day we have sung an Easter hymn and that I have just announced a proper Easter text when Easter Day is already five weeks past. In reply I would like to invite you to reflect upon this point, which no doubt not every one realizes, though every Christian should: every Sunday is in truth an Easter celebration. I regret to say that this interpretation of Sunday has almost disappeared from our field of vision because we have substituted our Sunday for the Sabbath observance of the Jews. We have been officially taught that the fourth commandment—"Remember the Sabbath Day to keep it holy"—means for us the Christian Sunday. But the Jewish Sabbath is not at all the same thing as the Christian Sunday. The Sabbath is in fact the last day of the week, a day of rest after six working days. And the essential point is that the primitive Christian community did *not* keep the Sabbath day, the seventh day of the week, but Sunday, the first day of the week. And they did so because the first day of the week is the day of the resurrection of our Lord Jesus Christ. Their Sunday festival was nothing other than a commemoration of the resurrection of the Lord, and so, in observing the first day of every week as the day of the Lord's resurrection, they really celebrated Easter each week.

It may not seem so very important in itself whether we celebrate the first or the seventh day; clever people may be eager to point out that it comes to the same thing in the end. Certainly, it is not so very important. But this Christian deviation from Jewish usage was the expression of a mighty fact, viz. that for the early Christians the resurrection of Jesus Christ from the dead, the Easter event, constituted the focal point and the essential matter of their faith. Had any one asked them what, in fine, their faith consisted in, they would have answered: "In this, that our Lord Jesus, the Son of God, the Crucified, is risen, and that we His disciples by faith in Him share in His resurrection and His eternal life. This is our distinctive possession, this is why we are so glad and why the Spirit of God dwells in us and accomplishes such powerful deeds among us. This is the eternal Spirit of the Risen Christ, the Spirit of life—of life eternal." The Gospel is essentially a message concerning the gift of eternal life.

We men of to-day live under the shadow of death. That is true not only of our own generation but of men generally in so far as they live without Jesus Christ. Man living by the light of nature lives as one who awaits death. We know nothing for certain about our future except this one thing: that we must die. This has always been so. But our generation has become in quite a special way conscious of the fact. The spiritual barometer of a period is always its philosophy. It was reserved to our own time to produce a philosophy of which the awareness of death is the central feature and in which life is characterized as a "*being unto death*", as inescapably orientated towards death. This statement in itself is trite and platitudinous. And yet this is the first time that such an observation has become the guiding thread of a philosophical system, for in former times the theme of death and its inevitability was always avoided. Our greatest German poet, Goethe, is an example of a man who studiously evaded the thought of death—and in that he was typical of his period. It was considered indecent to speak of death—as though the idea was: death comes soon enough when it does come, we won't spoil our lives now by thinking of it.

But to-day it has become impossible to adopt such an attitude. We can no longer be silent on this theme however painful it is. That is what I take to be the central significance of existentialist philosophy (so-called) in which life is viewed in its ineluctable connexion with death. It is simply no longer possible to shirk the fact, we must frankly say: yes, we are living in the presence and power of death and that is the essential meaning of our life. From this flows the consequence likewise emphasized in this philosophy: life has properly no meaning, it is at bottom vanity and nothingness. In Latin, nothingness is "nihil", and nihilism forms the distinctive characteristic and the programme of the fashionable philosophy of to-day. One may agree with it in so far as our life, if understood through its relation to death, becomes meaningless and vain. Death and nothingness belong together, for death is the great leveller and annihilator.

There are many reasons why this in particular is the keynote of modern philosophy. The most fundamental is to be seen no doubt in the two world wars and the fear of the imminence of a third, for war especially in its modern form is nothing else but a conglomeration of death, destruction and annihilation. But let us not deceive ourselves. Even without world war, death remains the visible ruler of this world. The well-known proverb which asserts that all roads lead to Rome would have to run, more accurately: all roads lead to death. And whatever man undertakes in order to elude this dreadful truth, it still remains clear that in the struggle of human enlightenment, knowledge, culture and civilization with death, death is triumphant. It is as if from the ends of the earth, death, like a wicked demon, surveyed man's desperate striving to evade him and mockingly rejoiced in the fact that all these human efforts, especially the noble art of medicine, at most served to postpone the inevitable moment when man would become his prey. Death remains the secure heir of all things: he is the universal inheritor against whom all testaments made with the purpose of disinheriting him are of no avail. In the last resort he seizes everything—individual lives and peoples, cultures and civilizations. Ultimately he devours everything with colossal insatiable appetite, with the result that destruction, nothingness, prevails.

At heart we all know this very well and from this source flow all our fears, cares and griefs. Our awareness of death and its terrible reality is the great dark shadow which overshadows the whole of human life and the life of every individual. Above all that we men are able to accomplish, there echoes the scornful mockery of death: all your human activity and effort are vain, in the end, I, nothingness, engulf everything. I am the universal inheritor.

And now let us read once again our text: "Blessed be the God and Father of our Lord Jesus Christ, who according to His great mercy begat us again to a living hope by the resurrection of Jesus Christ from the dead, to an eternal inheritance that fadeth not away, reserved in heaven for you."

Have you noticed how in this text, almost in the very same words, the opposite of these claims is asserted? Here too it is a question of an *inheritance* and of one that is ultimately valid, ultimately unchallengeable. The other term that we have used —the term *testament*—does not specifically appear, but is wholly relevant to the general meaning. Here someone has made a testament—but not we men: for our human testaments, however wisely made and legally secured, are of no avail to detract one iota from the universal inheritance of death, which in the end devours all. But here we see that One has made a testament which disinherits death and does so effectually and finally. Whoever is named in that testament escapes the power of death which otherwise unfailingly engulfs all things. Here a testament is made against death and one that secures to those whom it affects an incorruptible and undefiled inheritance that fadeth not away.

Now this is something very different from all those human endeavours of which we have been speaking, which are all inspired by the purpose of snatching something from the realm of death, but which nevertheless are all of such a character that death can mock at them, because in the end they must fail. These human treasures—material, cultural, political, social— are destined ultimately to fall a prey to all-devouring death. Hence such human acquisitions are transitory: they fade away. But here is a testament which death cannot mock because it does in fact deprive it of something, namely, of all those who are here made valid heirs.

All this sounds so incredible and unlikely that we must gain more precise information: how then does this testament come to be, who is the testator with power to disinherit death and what is the heritage which thus falls due? Our text supplies the answer to this very question: "Blessed be the God and Father of our Lord Jesus Christ." Thus He it is who makes an attack upon the present universal dominion of death. A still more powerful conqueror—the Almighty One—has come to undermine the all-conquering rule of death and has disinherited *it*. God is not only the Lord of all life, but the vanquisher of death. Of God alone can that be said; all the attempts to infringe and cancel the rights of inheritance exercised by death have failed. None has power over death except God: but He has slain this "last enemy".

And, moreover, we are plainly told who this God is—not a god conceived by the human mind and emerging from some system of ideas, not the god of some mystical religion. It is just in this matter that all these gods evince their ultimate power-lessness, and it cannot therefore be said of them that they offer any living hope. No, that God alone is the true God and van-quisher of death who is the Father of the Lord Jesus Christ. Hence He is the Author of the Testament and the source of the inheritance.

And now let us hear how this testament came into being. It is made operative thus: "*By the resurrection of Jesus Christ from the dead.*" In *that* event it happened that a mighty assault was made upon the kingdom of death. It is in fact the case that only one man has escaped the bondage of death. But this one man, Jesus Christ, is not just one man among other men, nor even simply an outstanding man. For is it not true that all the distinc-tions which we make between pre-eminent and commonplace men, between the great and heroic and the petty and undistin-guished, between the masses comprising 2000 millions and the elect few who tower above them all—that all these distinctions are useless in face of the universal Leveller? Death engulfs all, tirelessly, effortlessly. But this One—death could not hold Him. The Resurrection of Jesus Christ is an unconditionally unique event, as also Jesus Christ Himself was an unconditionally unique man: the God-Man, in whom God Himself was acting and speaking.

Of course this Jesus died visibly to all and died indeed upon the Cross. Again, this Jesus was buried. But the grave had no power to entomb Him: on the third day He rose again and showed Himself to His disciples, talked with them, even ate with them. The reports which we have of this event in the New Testament are not as a matter of fact completely consistent: but one thing stands out unassailably: the disciples saw Him, the Risen Lord, and He proved to them that He was the unquenchably living One. Therein lies the mighty fact of Easter; the mighty miracle of Easter. That happened on the third day after the crucifixion, on the first day of the week, and for that reason Christians have perpetually celebrated this first day of the week every time they gathered together for divine worship. This Sunday festival was for them a commemoration of that first Sunday, the Day of Resurrection, and thus should we Christians continue to celebrate and interpret Sunday. *This* is what is meant by the "Lord's Day".

This first Sunday is so important because it is the day on which the New Testament took effect. God then disinherited death and made heirs of eternal life all those who belong to the Lord Jesus Christ. He thus made heirs not only the Christians who were alive at that time, but all those, throughout all future ages, who were to believe on the Name of the Lord Jesus. You, my friend, are included in this testament if you believe on the Lord Jesus Christ.

This is what the apostle means when he says *"God begat us again unto a living hope"*. To believe in Jesus Christ means: to believe that this testament duly executed by Jesus Christ includes me. What now does the inheritance consist of?

The Bible employs several expressions to explain this, of which the most important are: the Kingdom of God and eternal life. We can speak only in metaphors about these truths because their scope lies not only beyond the limits of this world but also beyond the limits of our powers of understanding. But that does not prevent us from knowing them and their impact, even though we cannot conceptually represent them to ourselves.

Present

We apprehend the fact that Jesus, the Risen Lord, revealed the life of the world to come. This means life in communion with God, life in fulfilment and realization, in fact the life of God Himself in so far as He permits us to share it. It is the life from which death and sorrow, sin and transitoriness, are banished. To put it still more plainly: it is the life of perfect love, of the love which is the very being of God and which He alone can dower upon us.

Future

The fact that we cannot understand how these things shall be does not in the least prevent us from looking forward to them with rejoicing. We know that the best which already here on earth we can receive through Jesus Christ and do in reality receive, is life lived in love, in the power of the love of God, in the love for others which God sheds abroad in our hearts, life in communion with God and hence in communion with our neighbour. All this is a beginning and a foretaste of what is to be. We need not and should not wish to picture to ourselves the joys of heaven and of eternal life. By such attempts, we can only fall into the indulgence of fantasy. But we ought to know that it is the fulfilment of the end to which God has created us men. Not the fulfilment of all human wishes—for what folly lurks in our own secret desires—but the fulfilment of our deepest longings and our true destiny.

Now it is especially important that we should in fact live in looking forward to this perfect life, that we should truly cherish this hope with inward assurance. We can only do so if, just as we are to enter into the resurrection life of Jesus Christ, we also enter into His death. These two aspects are indissolubly linked together: it is impossible to have the one without the other! Whoever is not willing to die with Him, cannot live with Him either. But to die with Him means: to devote our lives to the service of others and to sacrifice our pride and self-righteousness by faith in Him, who for our sakes had to sacrifice His life on the Cross. Only through the Cross of Jesus could the way lead to His resurrection; only through our dying with Him can our way lead to resurrection with Him. The whole life of the Christian can be summed up in the two phrases: to die with Him, that we might live with Him. The latter is the goal and this goal forms the true content of the Gospel message. Hence as Christians we are called to be men who bear in their hearts the joy of Easter, hence men who lead their lives in this world, overshadowed by death, inspired by the joyful certainty of the Resurrection and of the life of the world to come.

CHILDREN OF LIGHT

For ye were once darkness, but are now light in the Lord: walk as children of light (for the fruit of the light is in all goodness and righteousness and truth), proving what is well-pleasing unto the Lord; and have no fellowship with the unfruitful works of darkness, but rather even reprove them; for the things which are done by them in secret it is a shame even to speak of. But all things when they are reproved are made manifest by the light: for everything that is made manifest is light. Wherefore he saith, Awake, thou that sleepest, and arise from the dead, and Christ shall shine upon thee.

Eph. 5: 8–14

ONCE you *were* such and such—but now you *are* otherwise. Thus the apostle addresses his Ephesian converts, and with justification. For at one time they were all heathen and led a heathen life corresponding with their idolatrous beliefs. Then the day came when they—not all simultaneously, but some at one moment, some at another—recognized the error of their heathen beliefs, when the light of Christ shone upon them, when they left old things behind them and stepped into the new world, the world of light and life, disclosed by Jesus Christ, expressing their conversion outwardly in the acceptance of baptism. So it still happens in the mission field. But it does not happen thus amongst us, here at home. Most of us, if not all, were baptized as babes in the first weeks of life, learned from our earliest years of Jesus Christ as Saviour, were instructed in this faith in Sunday School, in day school and in confirmation class—a faith which we have embraced from childhood as a matter of course. Perhaps too at the time of our confirmation we have openly professed this faith as our own. How then should that "once and now" of which the apostle speaks to his Ephesian converts find an echo in our lives? We have never been heathen, we have never experienced the transition from heathendom to the communion of Christ's flock. Before we ourselves were in a position to take any steps in the matter, we were already through baptism made members of the Christian Church. How then could we be aware of that gulf between the "once" and the "now" of which Paul speaks?

Exceptionally it is even found amongst us, in spite of our national Church. For there are not a few, who, although baptized when babies, have grown up without any regular connexion with the Christian faith and Church, since their parents themselves were without any such connexion. Still many more there are, who, although religiously instructed and confirmed, have subsequently completely lost all connexion with the Church and even with faith itself, have ceased to pray or to open their Bibles, or to enter a church; who thus have consciously refused to embrace Christianity, and have become deliberately and consciously irreligious. In fact we must no doubt consider that a great section of our people belong more or less to this class, although there are admittedly many intermediate cases, in that some wish at least to have their children brought up in the Christian faith, others themselves attend divine worship from time to time at the great festivals.

But among such as are thus quite estranged from the Christian faith, it may of course happen—and thank God it happens not seldom—that some day they are again struck by the impact of the Gospel and pass from their godlessness into an acceptance of the Christian faith, and further, no doubt, into membership of the Christian Church. To such the words of the apostle— "Once ye were—but now ye are" apply without further qualification. Perhaps some such are now among us, though they may well be quite a small minority.

Or, to mention yet again a third possibility: there are some who have never outwardly broken with the faith, who after their confirmation remained more or less church members, but who conformed only in an outward sense and for the sake of custom, until the hour came when they consciously became Christians and have regarded themselves as such only from that moment of illumination. For them too the words of the apostle about once and now are easily intelligible, for they too have experienced something of the same kind.

But for others of us who have never known such a sharp break with the past, because Jesus Christ from our youth up—no doubt in varying degrees—has been our acknowledged Lord and Saviour, whose disciples we have consciously been, for us this "once" and "now" in the sense which the apostle implies has never been a vital experience. In our lives, this break, this unique crisis of the twice-born, has never taken place, but instead we have known many of those conversions which, as Luther puts it, the Christian must experience afresh every day. We could not name any specific day or hour when we became the disciples of Jesus Christ. Instead of that, our inner lives show a graph of the process of Christian living which has its high and low points, or, as the physicists would express it, its maxima and minima. The life of faith, says Luther, consists not in being, but in becoming. That is what we would have to say about ourselves and also should say.

For does not the apostle have to reckon with this characteristic even in the case of his Ephesian converts who all of them became Christians by a clean break? He exhorts *them* also to enter once more into the light of life. Obviously they had not simply been abiding in that light which had nevertheless shone upon them when they became Christians. Indeed, he appeals to them thus: "*Awake thou that sleepest and arise from the dead*".... Those are strong terms to use in addressing such as already belong to the community of Jesus Christ, and especially in Ephesus, the outstanding centre of heathendom, where there yet stood the great temple of Diana or Artemis, a world-famous sanctuary to which every year hundreds of thousands made a pilgrimage. There the Christian flock represented a tiny minority and hence they must have been at pains to maintain their distinctive life.

Thus in spite of the fact that this community as a struggling and confessional Church must certainly have been alive, the apostle felt it necessary to challenge them with these words about arising from the dead, and from sleep. By this he makes it clear—what is our everyday experience—that our faith is no secure possession on which we can simply sit, as a man might say: "I have safely invested my millions and need not therefore bother any further about money." Faith is rather like a running stream, of which the water is fresh when drawn but becomes foul and stagnant when you let it stand. You must draw life from Christ every day anew, otherwise it becomes stale, impure and unreal, indeed ineffectual and dead. Just think how nonsensical it is—a life that is dead, a power that is ineffective.

Where then can we draw this water of life daily anew? Let us think over this question during our holidays—for as holidays should serve for the recuperation of our physical powers, so also they ought to promote the renovation of our spiritual life and faith. Whence do we derive the new life, the true life, the life in God? My friends, God has given us a *spring* from which we may draw the waters of eternal life. This spring is called *Jesus Christ.* "Whoever drinks of the water that I shall give him, will never thirst", for his soul's thirst is quenched with eternal life. But how can we contrive to draw this water of life from Jesus? If I am to express it in terms corresponding to the image of the cistern, I would say: we need for this purpose a vessel and we need a pulley with which to let it down. The vessel is faith. By faith alone can we apprehend Jesus Christ and eternal life in Him. And the pulley with which we let down the vessel is prayer. Many a time the vessel comes up empty because the rope was not long enough. We must take time over the business of drawing this water, by the reading of Holy Scripture or of some book calculated to enable us better to understand Holy Scripture or by that discourse with God which we term prayer. We can do that also on our walks, even aloud, so that our thoughts do not escape us; but I will not speak further of this at the moment.

In our text the apostle puts the point in another way. All our talk about God, about Christ, about eternal life, can, of course, only take place in figurative speech: in this realm there is no question of finding a formula in which the truth can be crystallized once for all. The figure which the apostle uses here is that of light. Walk in the light, not in darkness. We cannot ourselves generate the light, the salvation, the eternal light which is in Christ. But we can step into the light and leave the sphere of darkness. We can walk in the light and dwell in the light while we are conducting the affairs of our earthly life. That is very easily said. But what can I do? Step into the light! Each of us knows that there exists not only outer physical light but also *inner light*, just as there is an inner darkness as well as an outer one. When we are engulfed in darkness, then we ourselves are penetrated with gloom, it is gloomy within and around us. Our relations to our neighbours are overshadowed as are also our relations to our colleagues and friends and our affairs in general.

What are we to do when we are thus joyless, enwrapped in inner darkness, when everything seems to go wrong and our whole lives are twisted? Then there is only one resource: to step into the light and, as Paul expressly says, into the light of the Lord Jesus Christ. Then something remarkable happens. We notice in fact that this darkness has its origin entirely within ourselves. Whereas we supposed formerly that other people or our circumstances were to blame, in the moment when the light of Christ shines upon us, it becomes quite clear that *the source of gloom lies in ourselves*. It is my ego which constantly blocks the light. This ego is very opaque. Where it stands, it shuts out the light from others too. How often, my friends, have I blocked the light from others by my thickly opaque ego which thus casts a shadow everywhere. It is this ego which is the source of all darkness.

But the trouble is that we cannot simply get rid of this ego. What shall we do then? When we enter the light of Christ, a second truth dawns upon us. It is that our ego can become transparent, so that it no longer blocks the light from others, but on the contrary reflects the light of Christ. This is what the apostle means by "making manifest"—*everything that discloses truth is light*. This disclosure of truth takes place through confession. We must open ourselves to those from whom we conceal the light: then we become transparent vessels of the light of Christ. If there is something not quite right between us and other people—some element of opaqueness and obscurity—then when we step into the light of Christ we are impelled to confess the measure in which we are guilty and responsible. We candidly acknowledge our faults and all is well again.

Consider this, my friends. God did not give us our personalities that they should be full of themselves. God intends the ego to be only a *receptacle* which Christ is to fill. Paul expressed this on one occasion in striking fashion when he said—in exact correspondence with his experience: "I live, yet not I, but Christ liveth in me. The life which I now live in the flesh, I live by faith in the Son of God, who loved me and gave Himself for me." Nature had endowed the apostle Paul with a massively built ego; he was, as we say, a strong and compelling personality. In so far as he made his weight felt, he cast around him a dark and heavy shadow—we know of course how he persecuted the first Christians. But the day came when the light of Christ dawned for him, when he realized that Jesus Christ had been crucified for him, and once his soul was flooded with the light of that truth, he saw that he must enter into and share the crucifixion of Christ and that his ego must be slain; and when he surrendered himself to the crucified Christ who had died on his account—in that very moment it happened that his ego became transparent because it was no longer filled with a purely Pauline content but with the light of Christ—the eternal light of God. "But now it is no longer I that live, but Christ that liveth in me."

And from then on he became another man, breathing the spirit of mercy, righteousness and truth. From that moment onwards he could become a witness of Jesus Christ. For you cannot be a witness if you are dully opaque, if you plunge others as well as yourself into the shadows. You can only be a witness to Jesus Christ if you are willing to allow His radiance to be reflected from you. What miserably dim lamps are we preachers of the Gospel through whom the light of Christ but feebly shines, because we are still penetrated with an opaque egocentricity! And how dimly the light of Christ flickers in you members of the congregation because you too are so dominated by the ego!

You must understand aright what I am saying about the "ego". It does not mean that we must cease to be ourselves if we wish to become disciples of Jesus. For not everything about our personalities is opaque material. On the contrary our whole personality can become radiantly transparent without anything of our God-given distinct individuality being sacrificed. The opaque element is only the I which is incessantly self-concerned, self-willed, ambitious, susceptible, self-seeking, self-centred.

That is what I mean by the dark impenetrable self. How far is your ego healthy? That is the question which relentlessly challenges me when I face the light of Christ. As long as I refuse to consider this question or to answer it sincerely, I am hiding away from the light. Of course it is easily said, "We must step into the light of Christ", but it is not so easily done. But immediately we make a beginning with the process, the decisive question faces us: What is the condition of your inner self, at what point do you alone want to be in control, rather than allow me to be your Master?

We are to walk as children of light, as bearers of the light of life, penetrated with the radiance of Christ. This can only happen in so far as we become children of God. But we shall become such, only when we realize that all darkness and gloom has its source in ourselves and light comes only from God's forgiving grace. "He is thy light, O soul, forget it not!"—thus we sing. When we ourselves wish to be the source of light, then darkness entombs us: but when we recognize that in God alone is light, we too can become burning and shining lights. Yes, and we shall become such. In the moment when we confess our sins and receive absolution from Jesus Christ, we begin to become transparent, and the process increases the more we live in union with Christ through the reading of Scripture and prayer.

My friends, there are just now many of you who are about to go off on your holidays. May I urge you: Let these few days or weeks, in which you may enjoy tranquillity and repose, be used in such a way that the peace of God enters your souls and that you may return renewed as children of light. To those others, I know not how many, who must remain at home and work, or who perhaps have already had their holidays, may I say: holidays after all are not needed for that peace to descend upon us which is the pre-condition of our facing the light of Jesus Christ. We can have it every morning if only we will spare even a few minutes to pray and meditate on Holy Scripture.

But to all of you I say: "Step forth into the light that you may become children of light!"

"UNTIL CHRIST BE FORMED IN YOU"

And the angel said unto them, Be not afraid; for behold, I bring you good tidings of great joy which shall be to all the people: for there is born to you this day in the city of David a Saviour, which is Christ the Lord.

Luke 2: 10–11

My little children, of whom I am again in travail until Christ be formed in you.

Gal. 4: 19

THE words which the angel addressed to the shepherds in the field form part and parcel of our childhood memories with all their train of sweet and dear associations attuning us to quite a special disposition of peace and joy. But just because they are saturated with the whole magic of the Christmas festival, the danger exists that we regard this angelic message as belonging essentially to a world of romantic poesy and child-hood dreams, as something utterly incongruous with the real world in which adults must live, that rough, hard, brutal world of everyday life where we must dash into the sordid scramble for money, where sickness and death constantly overshadow us, and strike into our lives with terrifying suddenness, that hum-drum reality of which the newspapers give us their sombre reports, the world which forms the arena of a colossal struggle for power, of blood-shedding, of callous and bloody wars. It is noteworthy that the angel's first words are: *"Fear not!"* But our real world is to be sure a fearful world, not an idealized Christmas world. In the course of the last 1900 years it has not become less fearful, and above all in the last three or four decades there has been no escape from a nightmare of terror. Thus the Christmas narrative strikes upon our ears with far-away, child-

ish-sweet harmonies, but with such an air of complete un-
reality that it appears to us as something which perhaps once
was, as our childhood world of legend and wonder once was,
but which no longer *is*. This Christmas poesy does not at all fit
into a world of roaring furnaces and the hum of machinery, of
chambers where business leaders make their decisions, of conference rooms where the representatives of capital and labour
haggle over wages, of departments where decisions are taken
which affect the issues of peace and war. No! it does not hang
together!

But, see now! the words of the angel: "Fear not, for behold
I bring you good tidings of great joy" were specifically addressed to the very heart of this dark and terrible world. And it
is expressly said that this message of great joy shall be to all
people, to the whole of suffering humanity and men whose
hearts are failing them for fear. Furthermore, it is not a poetical
speech nicely calculated to weave a dreamlike world of infinite
beauty in which art can flourish, but it is the announcement of
a real, historical event, of something which has taken place with
all the irrevocable actuality of the things which we read about
in our newspapers and history books. It is quite simply true that
Jesus Christ was born, that He grew up as a carpenter's son in
Nazareth of Galilee, alongside four brothers and some sisters,
that after His baptism by John He went about through the
country healing all manner of diseases, and preaching the
gospel of the coming and already embodied Kingdom of God,
that finally He was arrested by the leaders of the Jews and pub-
licly crucified on Calvary by the Roman authority, and in the
end was seen by His disciples as the Risen Lord. All these are
indisputable *historical facts* which took place in the same world
in which the Roman Empire grew to power and finally collapsed, in which other world empires rose and fell, in which the
never-ending struggle for power and riches goes on still to-day.

But you will not find it recorded in the history books that
this Jesus of Nazareth is the Saviour of the world, that God has
rent the heavens and come down to seek our lost humanity,
that eternal light has broken in upon the darkness of human
history, that the hiddenness of the eternal almighty God who

reigns in sovereignty over the events of time was then revealed as the infinite and unconditioned love of the Father, that in the man Jesus the Son of God came to visit us, and that His life, death and resurrection signify the incomprehensible, unique, event of the atonement and redemption of the whole world. In world history we do not find anything of this dimension—an event which takes place once for all, which happens in time for all eternity. The process of world history resolves itself into the history of the unceasing mutations which the world undergoes, and its characteristic is that everything which happens and has happened on that plane may well have enormous consequences and produce tremendous and fateful changes—but there, in the sphere of world history, nothing happens of which we can say: this is unique in that what has now happened has decisive significance for all eternity. What we find rather in the time process is that one great event in the series is simply the outcome of others, exactly as in the lives of individual men, where everything comes to an end and finally all is swallowed up in the nothingness of death, beyond which there is no issue leading from the events of time into eternity.

In contrast to this, what happened in Jesus Christ flows from eternity, belongs to eternity and leads to eternity. For this reason, in contradistinction to everything, even the greatest and most significant of earthly events, it is *unique, once-for-all in character*. No doubt we are tempted to say: yes, but that too happened once, long ago. . . . Indeed, 2000 years ago it took place, and thus lies far away in the dim past, almost as distant as the history of Julius Cæsar and of Alexander the Great, almost as shadowy as the times of the Egyptian Pharaohs. All that belongs to the dead past; of what concern can it be to us in the living present? But the Word of God makes answer: what then happened has significance for to-day. That event is just as alive and decisive for every man and woman of to-day as it was for the disciples who walked with Jesus over the plains and hills of Galilee. Why so? Because in that event eternity, the eternal world of God, disclosed itself as the world to which we, too, we of to-day, belong through Jesus Christ. Then, in what happened in Bethlehem, in Nazareth, in Jerusalem, your eternal destiny was decided. For in the life of God is that joy and peace of which the angels sang, and you, too, in the present hour, are called to share that plenitude of life and joy and peace which is in God. The testament, decisive for your eternal future, was then sealed with the blood of the Son of God, and made valid for all eternity, and by this testament you are made an inheritor of the divine glory, of eternal fullness of life. "For God so loved the world, that He gave His only begotten Son, that whosoever believeth on Him should not perish but have everlasting life."

On earth, too, in our everyday life, testaments are made which can be of great importance in a man's life. But everyone knows how uncertain are these testaments drawn up and signed by men. Even when countersigned by a notary, all sorts of subsequent modifications may arise. The testator may take it into his head, only a few hours before his death, to make void this apparently so secure will, and to compose quite a different one. But this sort of thing cannot happen with the testament that is sealed by God in the blood of Jesus. It remains valid and unchanged for all eternity, and nothing can cancel it, neither the vicissitudes of fate, nor death. What then happened was unique, of eternally decisive import. You are made an heir, an heir of the divine glory, if only you do not mislay this testament, if only you abide in faith in that Word which God has given for all eternity and will keep.

We sometimes hear it said of a man that his future is assured. But that kind of thing is only broadly and approximately true: in reality no man's future is assured in the sense in which we now mean. How many have been forced to realize that, in these years of revolutions and world wars. They thought their future was solid and unshakeable and then it turned out so very differently. They supposed their future happiness was consolidated and then it crumbled away, often in a few seconds. In spite of all our established arrangements, we know nothing certain about our future. But in the testament of God, we read: "... that neither life nor death, nor things present, nor things to come ... can separate us from the love of God which is in Christ Jesus our Lord." We know that and we know it for certain because Jesus Christ is more than man, and His pledge is not merely human, but is the Word of the eternal God Himself.

Thus it is that what happened 1900 years ago is *decisive for to-day* for each of us, who is assured of this knowledge by faith. We can have secure information about our future as a result of what happened in that distant past.

Hence our life in the present assumes a different character. To-day we can be aware of eternity and of universal redemption. As a result of this present awareness, our experience to-day is penetrated with joy. Hence, in the midst of a terrible and dark world, we can be glad and radiant. That is the essential meaning of the Christmas festival and the Christmas joy.

But, further, our text from the Epistle to the Galatians says yet more about our life in the present, which we must briefly consider.

A line of the poet Angelus Silesius, whose real name was John Scheffler and some of whose poems are to be found in our church hymn-book, runs: "Were Christ born in Bethlehem a thousand times and not in you, you would be eternally lost." Thus he speaks of a birth of Christ to-day, in your heart. The Bible does not express this precise thought but we find in the apostle Paul something similar. "I am in travail until Christ be formed in you." Thus we are not merely to apprehend by faith the Saviour and what He once wrought for our eternal salvation; it is rather that to-day, in this our earthly life, *Christ must be formed in us*. This is a very extraordinary manner of speech. The apostle suggests that he suffers birth-pangs until in the inner life of the Galatian Christians the Lord comes to birth. A mother suffers birth-pangs when the new life that she bears in her womb is to be born into the world. Thus it would seem that the Christ-life now becoming manifest in the Church was at first generated in the heart of the apostle and on its account he must suffer the pangs of giving birth. This is a bold metaphor: and so much the more bold as it is a man who is speaking. But it must not be written off as a mere far-fetched image. The Christian life which is to flower in others is actually, at the moment of his writing, fully blooming only in the apostle himself, in whose heart it has come to be through the action of the Holy Ghost. And yet it is already germinating, though concealed, in the Galatian Christians: until it comes visibly to the light of day, much care and toil is needed on the part of Paul the pastor. But it must one day come forth as a divinely generated plant, as adoption into the sonship of God and hence also as likeness to Christ. Jesus Christ is, in the thought of the apostle, "the first-born among many brethren". What became fully manifest in Him as the resurrection life of Eastertide, must one day become resplendent also in the lives of believers.

Thus we are here very close to what the poet expresses: "Christ born in us." There must really take place in us something corresponding to what once happened in Bethlehem: a birth through the Holy Ghost. In other parts of the New Testament this process is in fact called "birth", a birth from above, or *a being born again*. This is what is meant. Through the gospel of Jesus Christ and the faith of the believer, a new man must come into being, a man in Christ, and this new life is not intended to be merely inward, but to manifest itself outwardly and bring forth its appropriate fruits. This new birth is the real implication of the Christmas festival, for only when this happens does the unique event of Christ become our property, our own life.

Jesus Christ has been given to us in order that a transformation may come about in our lives. Merely to believe in Him without anything new coming to birth in us, is a sort of belief which the Bible does not recognize as true faith. Faith in the true sense of the word means: to become a new creature. "If any one is in Christ, there is a new creation." To believe means: to be taken up, incorporated into the eternal life of Christ and to grow therein. This generation of new life is something transcendent and unique, namely this, that Jesus Christ begins to take possession of a human life. Yet the manifestation of this new element does not take place all at once, but by a process of inner *development*. This is what Paul means when he alludes to structural growth. He has spoken in greater detail about it in the fourth chapter of the Epistle to the Ephesians. There he says: "Speaking the truth in love, we must grow up in all things into

Him who is the Head, Christ, unto a fullgrown man, unto the measure of the stature of the fulness of Christ."

We are all very far from the attainment of this goal. No doubt there are among us men who by their joyful faith and the fervour of their love and the purity of their hearts bear magnificent witness to Christ: men in whom we see the very image of Christ. But these are very few even among us Christians, nay, even among those who have really been gripped by Christ and are being impelled by His Spirit. If the apostle were to come among us, he would be driven to say all the more earnestly that he suffers birth-pangs on our account until Christ be formed in us.

Two things above all hinder our spiritual growth. On the one hand, our fretful concern about the state of our soul's health, and on the other, our self-seeking impulses which in spite of all our prayer and meditation on God's Word, in spite of all our attempts at self-improvement, ever lurk within us, driving us to take ourselves more seriously than God, to consider our honour as more important than the honour of God, so that our pride refuses to bend beneath the yoke of the humility of Christ. As long as we are thus worldly and self-willed, Christ cannot take form and shape within us. There is no room for Him. Our souls are blocked by the pressure of the world and of the self. If we do not begin to make ourselves of no account, then our Christian life will inevitably be impoverished.

Let me then in conclusion invite you thus: Open wide your hearts to the message of Christ! Take seriously this word "Fear not!" For Christ's sake, give access to the Spirit of Christ who reduces our ego that He may be formed in us: for just by that means, and only so, do we ourselves become what God has intended us to be: true-hearted men, men of love, men who do not seek their own but the good of others, men who have the mind of Him "who though He was rich, yet for our sakes became poor". In order that we may thus be renewed, we need recollection and tranquillity. Let us use this Christmas Day so to receive Christ in the silence and in our hearts, that we ourselves become, what He is in His divine mode: "children of light".

THE LAST HOUR

But when the Son of Man shall come in His glory, and all the angels with Him, then shall He sit on the throne of His glory: and before Him shall be gathered all the nations: and He shall separate them one from another, as the shepherd separateth the sheep from the goats: and He shall set the sheep on His right hand, but the goats on the left. Then shall the King say unto them on His right hand, Come, ye blessed of my Father, inherit the kingdom prepared for you from the foundation of the world: for I was an hungred, and ye gave me meat: I was thirsty, and ye gave me drink: I was a stranger, and ye took me in; naked, and ye clothed me: I was sick, and ye visited me: I was in prison, and ye came unto me. Then shall the righteous answer Him, saying, Lord, when saw we thee an hungred, and fed thee? or athirst, and gave thee drink? And when saw we thee a stranger, and took thee in? or naked, and clothed thee? And when saw we thee sick, or in prison, and came unto thee? And the King shall answer and say unto them, Verily I say unto you, Inasmuch as ye did it unto one of these my brethren, even these least, ye did it unto me. Then shall He say also unto them on the left hand, Depart from me, ye cursed, into the eternal fire which is prepared for the devil and his angels: for I was an hungred, and ye gave me no meat: I was thirsty, and ye gave me no drink: I was a stranger, and ye took me not in; naked, and ye clothed me not: sick, and in prison, and ye visited me not. Then shall they also answer, saying, Lord, when saw we thee an hungred, or athirst, or a stranger, or naked, or sick, or in prison, and did not minister unto thee? Then shall He answer them, saying, Verily I say unto you, Inasmuch as ye did it not unto one of these least, ye did it not unto me. And these shall go away into eternal punishment: but the righteous into eternal life.

Matt. 25: 31–46

THIS tremendous parable concerning universal judgment immediately precedes the passion narrative in the New Testament. Let us then consider it on the threshold of Passiontide and reflect upon the message it bears for us. It is a Scriptural theme which more than any other has been plastically presented by painters and sculptors. Again and again we find on the doors and in the interiors of medieval cathedrals this picture of the final judgment of the world, with the blessed on the right hand, the cursed on the left, and over them both the world's Judge with His sword. The artists thus suggest that there exist these two spheres—heaven for the blessed and hell for the reprobate. *There are*—the emphasis is on those two little words —such as are saved and such as are damned.

But, my friends, every time that in sermons or church teaching that simple phrase "there are" occurs, we can be pretty sure that something has gone wrong. Of course these scenes sculptured in stone on the doors of our churches, representing on the right hand the felicity of the saved, and on the left the lamentations and despair of the accursed, make this interpretation of the theme particularly impressive. We see embodied before our very eyes these two ultimate goals—heaven and hell. But precisely in that approach lies concealed a distortion of Christ's Word. Those pictures and this parabolic speech of Jesus appear to say precisely the same thing and yet they say something quite different. Jesus does *not* say: "there are these two spheres." Jesus does *not* make men spectators of a universal stage on which they watch what is happening to the two contrasted groups. Jesus just does *not* do what 1200 years later the great poet Dante was to do in his *Divina Commedia*, i.e. divide humanity into such as go to heaven and such as go to hell. That is a medieval, or one might say, broadly, a traditionalist-ecclesiastical misunderstanding. The Lord Jesus refuses to make us spectators who with alternating compassion and joy behold in sympathy and imagination the drama of ultimate divine judgment, but in this parable He turns to each one of us whoever we are, Christians or Jews or heathen, believers or unbelievers, virtuous or vicious, cultured or uncultured. *You*, whoever you may be, are addressed, for here it is a question of you, of your decision and your eternal destiny. It is not: heaven and hell objectively exist, but: before you lies this *twofold possibility*. Let us now consider this approach in greater detail.

The theme of the parable is the Last Judgment, the End, which lies beyond all earthly history and all our human experiences in this world. Do not forget that nothing—whatever it be—which happens in this temporal earthly life—whether things go well or badly with you, whether you have success or failure, whether you attain your objectives or not—is ultimately decisive. The ultimately decisive, as opposed to the merely provisional, the merely intermediate stages, the absolutely valid and therefore solely important criterion, is disclosed in the *final goal of history*. To this all is moving, not only your individual life but the life of nations and of humanity as a whole. And at this final goal stands Jesus Christ. We so glibly say: "The decisive thing is"... but that is not correct because what we have in view is only temporarily and apparently decisive. *He* is the One who *alone* is qualified to pass an absolutely valid judgment; by Him alone can it be determined, whether things are well or not, whether your life reaches the good end or not.

He is the Subject of the Gospel. Who He is and what He wills, God's Word declares to us. Who is He? He through whom God, the Creator of all things, calls you to Himself and prepares for you and offers to you eternal life. He is the One who says that He will reject no one of those who come to Him. He it is who says: "Come unto me all ye that are weary and heavy laden and I will give you rest"; who says of Himself, "I am the resurrection and the life. Whosoever believeth on me will not walk in darkness but will have the light of life." He is the Saviour of the world who wishes to be your Saviour too, and never ceases to call you to Himself and to His eternal plenitude of life. He is the One who became man and gave Himself to the death of the cross in order that His divine love might reach you. He stands at the final goal, with His judgment that determines your eternal destiny.

It is not true that God has a dual counsel according to which He has created and eternally predestined some to blessedness, others to torment. The Scripture says nothing of that, not even one word. The counsel and world plan of God revealed in Jesus Christ is solely salvation, eternal life, the kingdom of God, the consummation of all things in Him and through Him. *That* is the Will of God—and this will is therefore not, as some are again teaching to-day, both good and evil, the good life and corruption. The will of God from all eternity is life and health and peace, the well-being and perfecting of all His creatures. For this good end and for nothing else did He create them. He wills and works solely for this fulfilment of all good. And this message He announces to you, sinful man, in Jesus Christ. He wills to forgive you all your sins, to heal all your infirmities. Whoever you may be, however things stand with you, however crooked the course of your life may hitherto have been: that and that alone He discloses to you as His plan and eternal will in Jesus Christ.

But He does not proclaim this with the implication—as many wrongly suppose—that this eternal fulfilment will be your lot in any event, that you can do what you will, it will be all right in the end. You may believe or not believe, be faithful or unfaithful—it is of no ultimate consequence: Christ will make you and every one blessed in the end. No, the Bible does not say this. The Lord Jesus Himself does not say so, certainly not in this parable. Rather He presents Himself here as the One who judges and by whose judgment all things are ultimately determined. *Decision*, not security in any event. Take note of that and decide now to live for Him, if you want to end well and not badly. The Gospel of Jesus Christ is not automatically universalist, guaranteeing salvation to all, in any event. The Greek word *krisis*, which means to discriminate and decide, has also the meaning "judge". Thus at the end of all human paths stands the Son of Man as *Judge*. The same Jesus Christ who forgives all your sins, who died for you, who for your sake assumed the form of a servant, that He might come near even to you—He is the One who is the sole Author of this ultimate discrimination. One cannot usurp eternal life in defiance of Jesus Christ. He alone is the Door which gives access to the kingdom of the Father, and if we do not pass through this Door we shall pass through the wrong door into the wrong place.

Now many of you will object: this is creating panic and alarm, and what good can come out of that state of mind? It is, they will say, the old-fashioned nauseatingly familiar preaching of hell, by which it is attempted to drive poor terrified mortals into heaven. My friends, these modern psychologists have not yet learnt the ABC of psychology, since they cannot distinguish between panic and serious-mindedness. Jesus Christ terrifies no one; on the contrary, He tenderly invites every single human being to His great supper and marriage feast. But of course if you do not accept this invitation because you have no time for it, not even time to pay any attention to it, if you consider anything and everything as more important than Jesus Christ and His message of salvation, then naturally you are running on the wrong track and are heading, not for blessedness, but for disaster. I am not saying this because I am one of those sadistic and cruel hell-fire preachers, but rather it is Jesus Christ Himself who warns us thus in almost all His parables and discourses and with quite special emphasis in this particular parable. He warns us just as the Bible as a whole does, as the prophets of the Old Testament and the apostles of the New Testament do. It will not do, my friends, simply to cut out this momentous word about decision and judgment, just because men do not want to hear it, because they maintain it is calculated to cause alarm which can do no good, and declare it is no longer in season and ought not to be preached nowadays. The Church is assuming a heavy responsibility in being silent about this aspect of things. I am afraid that so much of our preaching is vain and ineffective because so often we have not the courage to refer to this negative second point and wish always only to emphasize the first, the positive and consoling aspect.

But, I hear you say: there again goes the self-righteous Pharisee. You yourself belong of course to the saved, for you are a believer. It is other people, unbelievers, to whom you preach the doctrine of hell. This reproach is not without justification, unfortunately, and those pictures and carvings in our medieval churches all breathe something of this Pharisaic spirit, this ecclesiastical complacency and parsonic self-certainty. Yet in that precisely consists the misunderstanding, as I pointed out at the beginning. This parable of world judgment is not narrated for the benefit of "those over there" who are going to hell. It is addressed to *me* the preacher, and through me to you the hearer, whoever you may be. And now let us hear it from the lips of the Lord Jesus Himself who so delivers it that none can lull himself in self-righteous peace if he truly listens.

Jesus says indeed: everything depends on your relationship to Me—and on nothing else. I am He by whose judgment all is at the last determined. Hence in this parable He repeats, for example, the pronouns "I" and "Me" thirty times. Truly: His is the final decision. But in what way is the matter determined? Precisely not as the Pharisees imagine, or as they suppose who describe every sermon which refers to judgment as Pharisaic and self-righteous. No catechism is here made use of, in such a way that those who know all the answers and thus have the right beliefs are placed on the right hand, and those who fail the test and are shown to have wrong beliefs are relegated to the left. No mention is made of this sort of credal confession. Hence there is no word which might give rise to the ecclesiastical consciousness of security, expressed in the implication: we are the saved, for we belong to the true Church. It is rather that the sole and exclusive question is, what each man has *done*. And in this it is not a question of whether they were abstainers or vegetarians or socialists or capitalists, or whether they have contributed to this or that beneficent cause. It is clear that all that counts for nothing, one thing only matters: whether you have been *merciful* or unmerciful towards the men with whom you have had dealings.

"So then in the last analysis it comes to what we have always asserted and preached, quite apart from all Christian doctrine; the essential thing is our works of mercy! It is not faith that procures salvation, but deeds, good deeds. Not the true faith but the good deed is the decisive factor." My friends, that would be completely to misunderstand our parable. In that case a sharp and inescapable opposition would arise between Jesus and Paul, between the doctrine of justification by faith alone and that of justification by works. But there can be no question of this. Jesus Himself has completely obviated the possibility of such a misunderstanding for anyone who has ears to hear. Note well *who* receives the commendation "Ye blessed of my Father". It is precisely they who are unaware of their good deeds, those in fact who behave in accordance with that other word of Jesus, that the left hand should not know what the right hand doeth. Wherever *self-glorying* arises, whether it be ethical, or ecclesiastical-theological, or the complacency of possessing right beliefs, there is something seriously amiss. This parable is piercingly pointed precisely against the self-satisfaction of the righteous and secure, just as we find Paul saying: "Whosoever glorieth, let him glory in the Lord, that no flesh should boast before Him."

What separates us most decisively from God is self-righteousness, self-certainty, self-praise, self-satisfaction—that disposition to approach God with a claim: "God, you will surely acknowledge *me*, for you know who I am . . . I have, of course . . ." Whosoever thinks on these lines does not need God at all. He is justified by and in himself, he needs no Saviour, no Deliverer, he has already saved himself. Hence, in point of fact, Jesus, in this as in other parables, suggests the same truth as Paul in his doctrine of salvation not by works but by faith in Jesus Christ alone: salvation solely because Jesus, without our having any claim to recognition, acknowledges us as His own, with the result that we ask in astonishment: "Why ever should I be among the saved?"

This interpretation has exactly the opposite effect of the traditional medievalist approach to the parable. Indeed, these words of Jesus produce not self-certainty, but the complete dethronement of all human securities; they represent a frontal attack on the innermost centre of man's rebellion against God, on the thought: with *me*, things are well, there is no doubt that I shall attain my heavenly reward, but others whom I see around me will come to a bad end. Hence the aim of the parable is not to alarm. It is true that no good can come from fear and terror. Its aim is rather to mortify us and to shatter our pride, whether it be pride in our Faith, or in our Church, or in our virtue, or in our culture. For it is this pride which, like an insulator, divides us from God so that His spirit and His love cannot penetrate our hearts. When man really humbles himself before God, like the publican in that other parable who could but exclaim, "God be merciful to me a sinner!" then alone man draws near to God and God to him. Thus humility and love are always complementary, just as pride and relentlessness imply each other.

God sent us His Son Jesus Christ in order to proclaim to us God's purpose of gathering all mankind into ultimate salvation, to declare the joyful message of the final and absolute victory of God over all His enemies, the triumph of life over death, of love over hatred, of right over wrong, of peace over war. That is the consummation, the kingdom of God, eternal life. God invites us to share in that glorious kingdom through Jesus Christ. But two powerful obstacles hinder the acceptance of this invitation: on the one hand the indolence and frivolity which lead us to say—"It will certainly be all right, why need I make any effort?" and on the other hand the arrogance which boasts: "I am entirely competent to handle this business. I am the man for this job." In the presence of either attitude Christ with His gospel can have no place. The parable of world judgment rescues us from both, from the supposition that it will be all right anyway, and from the assumption that *I* belong among the elect in any event. Hence too this parable precedes the Passion narrative because it prepares the way for our acceptance of Him who died that we might live through Him.

JESUS IN GETHSEMANE

And they come unto a place which was named Gethsemane: and He saith unto His disciples, Sit ye here, while I pray. And He taketh with Him Peter and James and John, and began to be greatly amazed, and sore troubled. And He saith unto them, My soul is exceeding sorrowful even unto death: abide ye here, and watch. And He went forward a little, and fell on the ground, and prayed that, if it were possible, the hour might pass away from Him. And He said, Abba, Father, all things are possible unto Thee: remove this cup from me: howbeit not what I will, but what Thou wilt. And He cometh, and findeth them sleeping, and saith unto Peter, Simon, sleepest thou? couldest thou not watch one hour? Watch and pray, that ye enter not into temptation: the spirit indeed is willing, but the flesh is weak. And again He went away, and prayed, saying the same words. And again He came, and found them sleeping, for their eyes were very heavy; and they wist not what to answer Him. And He cometh the third time, and saith unto them, Sleep on now, and take your rest: it is enough; the hour is come; behold, the Son of Man is betrayed into the hands of sinners. Arise, let us be going: behold, he that betrayeth me is at hand.

Mark 14: 32-42

THIS is one of the most astonishing narratives in the whole of the Bible. To begin with, it is astonishing that *it should have come down to us at all*. Only those disciples who remained closest to Him had any knowledge of what took place in the Garden of Gethsemane on that last night. How easy it would have been for them to conceal the facts, and what good reasons they had to conceal them! For it hardly redounds to their credit but, on the contrary, puts them in a most ignominious light—this story of how they whom Jesus had chosen to be with Him in the hour when He most sorely needed their fellowship, basely failed Him in that supreme moment of agony. While He wrestled in a spiritual conflict such as no man before had experienced, they slept instead of praying with Him and for Him as He had expected. Even though, as far as they personally were concerned, they might have been prepared to expose their shame, yet out of regard for the young Christian communities they could well have judged it wiser to conceal this episode so as not to weaken the faith and zeal of those young Christians whose loyalty was so often to be put to the test. It is most surprising that despite all such considerations they did not withhold information about this shameful occurrence, just as Peter also did not attempt to hide the ignominy of his threefold denial of the Lord, but disclosed the facts although no witness was present who could have challenged him to do so. This truthfulness and humility on the part of the disciples in the confession of their own guilt is really astounding and we may add therefore— *en passant*—that we can be sure of the historicity of the scene, for to what motive could we attribute its subsequent invention?

But for a still more important reason the Gethsemane episode might have been concealed. The disciples, of course, proclaimed Jesus to be the Christ, the Messiah, the Son of God. But might not this story have awakened serious doubts as to the truth of this proclamation? Might it not for many believers have exposed Jesus to the reproach of weakness and unmanly fear of death? In point of fact we know that many Greeks and Romans mocked at this pretended Son of God, for they contrasted the Gethsemane incident with the accounts of the death of Socrates reported for us by his friends Plato and Xenophon. Socrates too had to die, had to drain the cup of poison which he knew would infallibly cause his death within a few minutes. But with wonderful serenity, with an almost incomprehensible cheerfulness of mind, he went through with the inevitable—and how favourably that attitude contrasts with Jesus' fear of death and desire to escape the cup of suffering. How very differently from Jesus Socrates proves himself to be a true hero—and in addition Socrates makes no claim to be other than an ordinary man. He is no Son of God. Thus the heathen mocked and were scandalized by Jesus—should not the disciples have foreseen this and suppressed the narrative? No one could have criticized them for so doing, because no one knew anything of the matter, and in any case they were not obliged to disclose all. It is indeed astonishing that this account should have reached us, so that every schoolchild knows of it wherever the New Testament is read.

But the element of surprise does not consist solely, nor even primarily, in the fact that the story has been preserved. It lies rather, in the first instance, in *the content of the story itself*, and it is this which I suggest for our meditation to-day in preparation for Good Friday.

Probably in no other story of the gospels does Jesus come so close to us as here. When it is affirmed in the creed of the Christian Church that Jesus our Lord became *true man*, of the same flesh and blood as ourselves, we find in this incident the most cogent proof of the tenet. "My soul is exceeding sorrowful even unto death", or, as others translate: "troubled and shattered as death approaches"—thus He speaks. And what is more human than such distress and agony and collapse? And further we read: "He began to be greatly amazed and sore troubled." There are people who would consider this attitude to be one of unmanly weakness, which should be overcome and which a brave man would easily overcome. In fact, there are men of heroic stature who never succumb to such fits of distress. For example, it is part of the moral code of the Japanese that a man, even when faced by death and undergoing the most terrible agonies of body or mind, should never betray his emotions, and many of them are in fact capable in such moments of keeping a smiling face as their law requires, and of never letting themselves go, as the expression is, of revealing no sign of pain or fear or distress. Was then Jesus weaker than these heroes? No, He was only more human: for that kind of self-control is at bottom only a matter of doing violence to one's own soul. That stoicism makes a man hard and that smile is, after all, false. God the Creator has not in vain given us men the gift of tears. Even we men must not be ashamed of weeping. Tears are not a sign of weakness, but a sign that we have a human heart: a sign that we were not created for apathy, but to experience both joy and pain in maximal depth and intensity. The true man is the man with a heart—it is just that which we see revealed in Jesus and we do not shrink from and are not ashamed of His wrestling in an agony of fear. This is how the apostles understood the matter, as, for example, the author of the Epistle to the Hebrews who expressly writes: "He must in all points become like unto His brethren that He might be a merciful and faithful high priest: for since He Himself suffered and was tempted, He is able to succour them that are tempted." And we read further on in the same Epistle: "And in the days of His flesh, He offered up prayers and supplications with strong crying and tears to Him who was able to save Him from death, and thus He learned obedience."

Here then is the decisive proof of the humanity of Jesus: He was *tempted* and He *prayed* for deliverance. In these two features we see the mark of man's creatureliness, in contrast to the Creator-being of God. Our susceptibility to temptation is a consequence of our freedom in responsibility. God could have created beings who must quite automatically obey Him. But such creatures could not in any case have been men. God endowed men with freedom of will and He requires us men to do His will in the freedom of personal decision. But the price of such freedom is exposure to the assaults of temptation. The Lord Himself in this hour of agony speaks to His disciples about the ever-present pressure of temptation, warning them: "Watch and pray that ye enter not into temptation" as He bids us also pray: "Lead us not into temptation." This exposure to temptation belongs as unconditionally to the essence of human nature as freedom belongs to it. But temptation is the danger spot where it is in the balance whether we shall finally choose God or ourselves, whether we shall be obedient or sinful.

In what then did temptation consist for Jesus? In the fact that His wish that the cup might pass from Him, i.e. that He might not have to suffer death upon the cross, might prove stronger than His obedience to God. His prayer expresses the force of this temptation. In prayer lies the sole possibility of deliverance for man, the creature, assailed by temptation, the sole hope of rescue from the real danger of disobedience. When we pray, we subject ourselves to God. The prayer of Jesus, as reported to us by the evangelists, is astonishing in its sobriety and—if I may say so—its incredible precision and penetration. It expresses exactly what at this moment is at issue. Jesus can legitimately pray that the cup of suffering might pass from Him. I know that on more than one occasion He has predicted to His disciples the imminence of His suffering and death; but the issue is after all to be determined in the sovereign freedom of God. God can, if He wills, fulfil His plan by other means than the passion of Jesus. Jesus can legitimately ask God to spare Him this cup, because He adds—and this is the decisive point: "Nevertheless, not my will, but Thine, be done." By this spirit of submission, the temptation has been overcome. Jesus has subordinated His individual will to the Will of the Father. Many of our own prayers do not really deliver us from temptation because we are concerned only with the fulfilment of our own wishes, because with us the ultimate prayer is not: "Thy will, not mine, be done."

I would like just to touch briefly in passing upon the objection which many people, who think themselves clever, have urged against this narrative: How could the disciples have known the substance of Jesus' prayer when they were asleep? Such people do not notice that the report mentions only this one theme of the prayer of Jesus—it was probably a matter of the first words which they heard just as they were falling asleep. Such carping criticisms reduce themselves to nothing as soon as we examine them with precision. Thus they caught this key-note of the prayer of Jesus and correctly understood the implication of the Lord's admonition: "Watch and pray, for the spirit is willing but the flesh is weak." In the New Testament "the flesh" connotes always man in his sheer creatureliness, as unrelated to God, while "the spirit" on the other hand suggests man's orientation towards God.

Now remains to be considered the chief question: How does this incident affect Christ's status as Son of God—or, as the Church creeds express it, *His divinity*? Does not this article of the creed become questionable in the light of this so unmistakable disclosure of the humanity of Jesus? In this sense so-called free-thinking theologians have always understood the matter and this story of Gethsemane is particularly dear and significant to them. They argue: thus we see that Jesus was a man like ourselves and that is all there is to it.

Now—to us also who believe in Jesus, the Christ, the Son of God, this episode is of quite special importance. Jesus is not the Son of God in any way which is incompatible with His being also true man. But precisely in this incident He manifests Himself not only as true man, but as the Son of God, as the suffering Servant of God who gives His life for the redemption of humanity. For here it is not merely a question of Jesus' fear of death. Not because He must die was He amazed and sore troubled. But in the last resort His temptation was to doubt His Messianic vocation in view of His imminent death on the cross. He had received from God this mission: to embody the Kingdom of God upon earth and to ransom humanity from sin and death. In fulfilment of this mission He had lived and preached, talked with men and performed His mighty works. All this He did as the Saviour, condescending to the lowliest and most wretched, and through it all He sought not His own, came not to be ministered unto but to minister, to heal and to forgive sins with the full authority of God. Was such a life to have been lived in vain: was it to end in catastrophe, was God at the last to withdraw from Him divine powers? On the contrary. God willed to consummate and crown this life of humility, but with a crown that was fitting: a crown of thorns. It was an exaltation which, from the point of view of the actualities of human life, symbolized the most terrible humiliation—namely, exaltation to the cross, the gallows, the stake of ignominy and shame and torture reserved for the criminal. For this reason Jesus was tempted to resist such an end. He would not have been true man, if at the last He had not been tempted to rebel against such a cruel annihilation of His whole life's work.

But the moment of resistance is resolved in surrender. He does not escape this culmination, this climax to His ministry which God had foreshadowed to Him, this ultimate mortification. The hour of agony is past. Completely composed, serene and transcendent in majesty Jesus goes to meet His captors. Fully at one with the will of God, He allows the traitor Judas to work his will.

Yet another point in the story is of special importance. First, Jesus is accompanied by His disciples, then He withdraws and takes with Him the three chief disciples only: but then it is partly that He moves away from them, partly that by their spiritual weakness they fail Him, so that in *total solitude* He wrestles in this supreme struggle. He alone is able to endure temptation without falling into sin. He remains firm in harmony with the will of God, although that victory costs Him the shame and suffering of the cross, and lends to His life's work the appearance of an error and presumption which God is thus avenging. We do not know what else Jesus prayed in that fateful hour in Gethsemane, what other terrible fears He had to overcome. As ordinary men we cannot pierce this mystery, but, casting a retrospective glance at the cross and resurrection, we may in some sense divine that there, in awful solitude, a real combat with hell was fought out by Him, the sole righteous One. He alone understood what was at stake, He alone was the object of the assaults of the powers of darkness, He alone was the Victor in the power of God.

For these reasons, then, this story is preserved in the Gospel. It is intended to show us the costingness of the work by which Jesus Christ ransoms us from the guilt of sin and bestows upon us the certitude of eternal life. This redeeming work is not, so to speak, an "objective" atoning sacrifice as though God had demanded the life of His Son, in order that we might go unpunished. It is a *personalist* transaction in which Jesus voluntarily assumes His passion and atoning death; it is a real, thoroughly *personal*, victory preceded by a fearful conflict. There is here nothing quasi-magical, no divine mechanism, no delivering *Deus ex machina*; the personal element interpenetrates the entire story.

The narrative of Gethsemane is so precious to us because it implies that our salvation is the fruit of a real victory. It has been infinitely costing—the fact that we may now rejoice in the unconditioned love and loyalty of God. The Gospel is not simply a matter of *doctrine* but involves a series of real historical *events*. God is not quite simply near to us, He has drawn near, so near in fact that the divine and human have become fused, not only in the miraculous birth of a God-man, but in the drama of a real conflict and a real triumph, which a man of flesh and blood like ourselves has lived through and carried through to a victorious *dénouement*. Just as the history of humanity is a living tragedy and strife, so the work of our redemption is an actual dramatic event, wherein the powers of darkness have been really slain in and through a man like ourselves, but who was other than we, in that He was tempted like ourselves, but remained without sin.

So we meditate upon the Passion story not from any morbid interest in suffering, but because we perceive that through those events we are freed and ransomed from the daemonic powers. There takes place there, if I may so express myself, the decisive "break-through" in the fight against the realms of darkness. There it happens that the doors admitting to the sanctuary of God, to the Father's house, the doors which had been barred by sin, are torn asunder, so that we now have access to the Father. Jesus has opened the way to the Father by means of His entirely voluntary death. He has shouldered the burden of our guilt that we may now have communion in the love of God. We have now a God whom otherwise we could not have had or known, a God who understands us in all things and yet does not reject us. If the proverb says: "To understand all is to forgive all"—a very dangerous proverb—we have as a complement to it the eternal assurance of the message: We have a God who understands our hearts, who understands me also and from whom I must hide nothing, a God who shrinks from nothing, to whom I can confess all and who nevertheless does not cast me out.

Hence we may say: Our faith flows from the victory which Christ has won. "This is the victory that overcometh the world, even our faith."

SELF-EXAMINATION

Try your own selves, whether ye be in the faith; prove your own selves. Or know ye not as to your own selves, that Jesus Christ is in you? unless indeed ye be reprobate.

2 Cor. 13: 5

THIS is a remarkable and very special kind of text. If I may so express myself, it is an upside-down text. Usually in a Biblical text we hear the voice of God, we apprehend the Word of God, revealing to us the secret of His will and calling us away from our own selves and our busy self-preoccupation into communion with His own life. But this text invites us to look into our hearts and to search them that we may discover what is *in us*. Does this mean, then, that for once we are to become the theme of the preaching, and that the sermon will consist in making us, so impoverished and wretched, the subject of revelation?

I am very glad that this text is a word of the apostle Paul—that apostle who of all the Biblical witnesses most unequivocally proclaims to us the grace of God in Jesus Christ as the sole source of salvation, and who, by his doctrine of justification through faith alone, exhorts us as no other does to look away from ourselves and to focus our attention on Christ alone. He will therefore certainly know why for once he speaks to us in this way, and we can assuredly be confident that he has not suddenly lost sight of the whole object and centre of his message. It is clear that this exhortation to examine ourselves coheres with the doctrine of justification by faith. So let us try to understand it; indeed we cannot do otherwise if we are going to take the apostle at all seriously.

Christ is indeed the theme of this text too. This self-examination is concerned with faith, of course with faith in the grace of

God which alone saves us, and its object is to discover whether we have truly understood this preaching and made this message the fundamental inspiration of our lives. When the crews of two ships converse with each other by signalling, the last signal is always: "Understand?" and the other party must always answer: "Right." The apostle wishes to know whether we have understood his preaching about the Christ with our minds only or whether it has pierced our hearts. For is it not the case that a gospel which has reached only the surface of the understanding is a misunderstood gospel? For God is less concerned with our rational intelligence than with our heart. He wills that Jesus Christ should not only *be* apprehended by us, but that He should *apprehend* us, that we should allow Him to be the sovereign Lord of our lives. This is what He means when He asks if Jesus Christ dwells within us. He seeks to dwell in and rule our hearts, not only our minds and memories. God is not interested in whether we can recite by heart passages of the Bible and like industrious pupils be able to give an accurate account of it. A well-furnished Christian school satchel may be very desirable, but it is not God's main concern with us.

Let me now begin at the other end and consider the question of those who are outsiders to the Christian faith. They ask us: What is your faith all about? What does your belief sum up to? Does it make any difference to your life? Does believing make you a different man from what you would be without beliefs? My friends, these are very reasonable and justifiable questions. Why should we build churches, train and engage priests, edit hymn-books with great care; in short, create and set in motion the whole of our ecclesiastical machinery, if, all in all, no ultimate real good comes out of it? Is it really worth while being a Christian? Could you honestly reply: "Yes, I would certainly be a very different man without my religious beliefs"? I beg you to bear testimony sometimes to the advantages you claim to enjoy thereby so that we may see something of these benefits and may say: "Indeed, if that is the fruit of belief then you are right, it is truly worth while." Thus people desire from us some *account of our faith*, and it is significant that the apostle Paul agrees with them and desires from us exactly the same thing. Thus we are indeed constrained to give some account of ourselves.

But, my friends, we already began to do this even before I announced my text. Have you not just been singing: "How should I not sing to God and rejoice in Him?" Thus the testimony to *joy* is the first note which appears in our account. When four years ago I was with my wife in Bangkok in Siam, speaking to a crowd of young people—mostly students—and, later, questions were invited, the first bashful question of a girl was: "Why do you seem so happy?" Of course, I was delighted to hear this unexpectedly naïve and personal question and gladly answered from the bottom of my heart, telling her about the God of grace who does in fact make glad the believer who trusts in Him. I can only feel shame that I do not any longer seem quite so happy. For to know the God revealed to us in Jesus Christ makes our hearts glad indeed, and if this joy were entirely foreign to us, we should invite the criticism: Your faith cannot go very deep: perhaps it is lodged only in your understanding and has not yet penetrated your heart.

Closely connected with the note of joy is that of *gratitude*. My friends, is it not the case that when you pray in the morning or the evening, the first word is always: "I thank Thee, O Lord"? Even when things are not well with us, when we have anxieties, cares, and sorrows—even then our first and ever-recurrent theme is thanksgiving. Most of all I thank God for the fact that He has given me grace to believe and that by this faith I can come to know God as my Father, and can realize that my life is in His keeping, that I may always and in every situation come to this God and talk with Him, lay before Him my cares and sorrows, which are greatly eased by that very fact.

But in praising God something else becomes manifest. We come to realize His omnipotence and holiness, His majesty and unimaginable greatness, and we are rapt in wonder and struck with *awe* and impelled to bow in adoration. We become aware that there is One above us and above all men, and all things. This knowledge gives to our subjective experience a new and immense broadening and deepening. By recollecting the greatness of God, much suddenly seems insignificant to us, which previously had loomed so large. So much becomes unimportant which before had preoccupied us unduly. This gives us spaciousness and freedom so that the cares of life do not press upon us and entangle us so much.

And in praising God we think of the goal which He sets before us. There are many people to-day who say that life has no meaning and is hardly worth while. That attitude is only possible because such people do not know God and thus have no eternal purpose by which their life can be shaped. When we affirm in our creed: "I believe in the resurrection of the dead and the life of the world to come", what we are saying is just this—"My life does not dissolve in nothing, and the life of humanity, to which I integrally belong, does not dissolve in nothingness, but it is orientated towards the Eternal, the Kingdom of God, and I, unworthy that I am, have received from Jesus Christ my Saviour the assurance that I shall have a share in this eternal life." That faith exalts our life above and beyond its perishability and nothingness. Such a faith is indeed the counterblast to the terrible modern philosophy of despair, to nihilism, and the existentialism that is akin to the latter. I know why I am in the world and why I am not journeying into the void: I know the goal that is set before me.

In this stocktaking process there appears much that we do not normally think of. To know why we are in the world is something extraordinarily momentous. Of course, many Christians seem not to know it, although it stands out in big headlines throughout the Bible. We are in the world to love God and our neighbour. That is our main business, whether for the rest we are tradespeople or scholars, farmers or industrial workers—all this that we are accustomed to describe as our business is only secondary. The primary vocation is the same for all of us: it is to love God and our neighbour. This realization gives to each day its divine meaning. To fulfil this gives us more than enough to do each day, although the fulfilment of it does not hinder us from our so-called business, for no special time need be set aside to love God and our fellow-men; it is a vocation which is woven into the texture of everyday affairs. Whether we are really fulfilling this main duty is another matter about which I propose to say something in conclusion. But to be aware of this true end and meaning of our life is something of immense significance for which we ought to thank God.

What else comes out in our stocktaking? If we believe in God the Father of our Lord Jesus Christ, then we know that our life is not governed by chance but by the will of God. If we look only to the things that are seen we can be greatly afraid in this world of ours. We do not understand the pattern of things, we do not know why it should be so and not otherwise, everything seems so fortuitous, so senseless and heartless, often so cruel, as if malicious mocking powers ruled the world or as if everything depended on purely mechanical causation. By faith, however, we know that this is not so. No hair falls from your head without the will of your Father in heaven, indeed all things must contribute to your ultimate blessedness—so the Heidelberg Catechism affirms: and so the Bible affirms, from which the former is drawn. Without faith we drift like lost souls in this world of chance, but by faith we know that we are securely *anchored*, not in the world as such but in the love of Him who controls the world.

What else do you find in the treasury of faith? One of the most important things of all: by faith I know that I am not my own master, but am ruled by a Master to whom I owe an account. "Whether we live, we live unto the Lord, whether we die, we die unto the Lord; whether we live or die, we are the Lord's." Nowadays men often live as though they were their own masters. They call this freedom. This philosophy of freedom is the very climate of the modern age. The message of this philosophy runs: Be free and therefore do not believe in the existence of God, otherwise you will be in bondage, and you will no more be free. This has been the teaching of Marx and Nietzsche and many others and humanity has believed them. What has been the result? Every man does what he wants and hence gets in the way of the other fellow, and thus arises universal strife. If there is no Lord over us, there can be no order, nor peace among men. But because I know that I belong to God, a controlling purpose and structure emerges in life. What then are we to think of this talk about freedom? We recognize that this modern doctrine of freedom is one big swindle. For the man who is his own master is not at all free in reality, but is a slave of his desires, his caprices, his sudden ideas, his moods, his passions. In faith we come to see that man is not made for this sort of freedom, freedom *from* God, but for freedom *in* God, by which he becomes free indeed. Just consider the people of your acquaintance: which of them give you the impression of being truly free? Precisely those who do not claim to be their own masters, but who own a Master. This allegiance renders them trustworthy, responsible and really free.

But now to turn to the direct question of the apostle Paul: "Know ye not as to your own selves that *Jesus Christ is in you*?" Jesus Christ is the heart and centre of our faith. It is, of course, through His mediation that we have all the blessings that I have been talking about so far. But I have not yet mentioned the most truly characteristic thing that we owe to Him—viz. *the forgiveness of sins*. That no doubt is something which those outside the pale of the faith do not understand at all, nor can they grasp its importance and centrality. But we think otherwise. Once we have recognized that the meaning of our life consists in our loving God and our neighbour, then we soon perceive that, measured by that criterion, we are miserable failures. If we are honest, we shall admit that we love ourselves more than our neighbours. And we love the world, good fortune, money, honour and health more than God.

So then we perpetually miss the mark in this business of living? Yes, indeed. It is this missing of the mark which the Bible sums up by the much-abused word "sin". We fail in the whole purpose of our lives because we love ourselves and the world more than we love God and our neighbour. Not only do we fail to fulfil the meaning of our lives, but we evade the divine will and command. And then it cannot but be that God Himself is obscured from us, that He is as it were distorted for us by our sin, so that we can no longer rightly speak with Him and trust in Him. Our faith threatens to lapse and we are faced with the danger of losing all those inestimable benefits which I have been summarizing. We fall into a state of dispeace with ourselves and our fellow-men, because we are no longer at peace with God. In this situation the phrase "forgiveness of sins" assumes a decisive significance for us at once. Can you or can you not believe that God forgives you your sins? That we might have the opportunity of really believing it, God has sent His Son that He might bestow upon us the forgiveness of sins through Him, through His entrance into our sin-sick world, through His death upon the cross, and by this means we can gain the certitude of forgiveness.

Now this is something that we cannot very effectively include in our testimony to others, for outsiders would not understand it; for them sin means nothing, nor the forgiveness of sins. But the apostle Paul asks us this very question. "Do you really believe in the forgiveness of sins?" If you are one who every day thanks God that your sins are forgiven, then Christ dwells in you. Thus the challenge of Paul takes us back to the very heart of his message about the sole sanctifying power of Grace. The interior self-examination here leads to an unusual result. Paul wishes to know precisely this: are you one who in this central concern of the Gospel does *not* dare to examine himself —otherwise he would find within his heart nothing but sin? If, on the other hand, your gaze is really focused on Christ, then you will find Christ within. Here we have reached the point where we cannot properly disclose to others what the faith means to us and how it benefits us, for they would not understand. We, however, know that just here lies the heart and centre of our faith and of the Biblical message.

Only from this point of view may I answer the question which for the enquirer is perhaps the most important of all: "Are you Christians really better than other people?" It is not legitimate for us to answer it: for if a man were to answer confidently: "Yes, I certainly am better" . . . he certainly would *not* be better, for he would not have understood Christ. But perhaps we may hope that others will bear testimony to us and say: "Indeed, he is no saint, but one notices that there is a something about him which is absent from other people—perhaps gratitude, perhaps humility, perhaps also a ray of that love which one cannot create oneself, but which Christ alone can bestow."

And one further point. As Christians we are differentiated from non-Christians by something which we *cannot do*. If the Christian faith really inspires you, and you seriously pray the Lord's Prayer, then you cannot be irreconcilable towards a man who has done you harm. When you come to the petition: "Forgive us our trespasses as we forgive them that trespass against us" and wish to receive God's mercy, then you must also forgive the sin of him who has done you wrong.

In conclusion, let us sum up thus: Yes, you outsiders, we have many inestimable benefits to show you which we gain through believing and would not enjoy apart from belief. Yes, it is worth while to believe, so much so that we can honestly say: only through faith does life take on for us its real value and meaning. In fact we may go so far as to confess with the Heidelberg Catechism: "That faith is our only consolation in life as in death."

"I AM"

Jesus saith unto him: I am the way, and the truth, and the life: no one cometh unto the Father, but by me.

John 14: 6

HAS it ever struck you how many sentences in the Bible begin with "I", especially "*I am*"? In the Old Testament it is the living God, the Covenant God, Yahweh, who so speaks: in the New Testament, in the Gospels, it is the Lord Jesus. Of course this is no accident, on the contrary it is extremely significant. In our ordinary human life, too, the word "I" is the word of capital importance. How many of our sentences begin with "I"—and not only sentences which we articulate aloud, but above all sentences which remain at the stage of thought. "I"—that is after all primary, that is our fundamental concern. Yes, and how could it be otherwise? To any one who has once grasped the full implications of the word I, it appears quite natural that this "I" should stand first and above everything else. I aspire to live, I want to enjoy prosperity, I want to be honoured and loved. And when we think about it, this point of view seems inevitable. We may say, of course: I am, after all, only an infinitesimal point in the whole world, which is so infinitely greater than I, yet at the same time I am the mind which is able to appreciate that disproportion and reflect upon it. We may also argue: humanity or my nation is so much greater than I, I am only one of many millions, of what significance can my individual life be? But again it is my mind which is thus able to measure and contemplate that contrast. This self-consciousness is a great mystery, it is not comparable with anything else in the world. It is, whether one realizes it or not, wishes it or not, the axis upon which the world revolves (*my* world, *my* people, the human race to which *I* belong), and it

173

furnishes also the supreme vantage-point from which we can survey and estimate all things. You may try desperately to persuade yourself: others are just as important as I myself, and because there are myriads of other people who are just as important as I, therefore I am not after all as important as I appear to myself. That is easily said; but it is not really so fundamentally. Other people are like figures on the screen of your private universe. You are the interpreter who determines what degree of importance they shall have. It is for you to decide what your relationship with them shall be. You must be clear in your own mind about this: you are once and for all—and you cannot alter the fact—the *centre* of your own world, even if every one else is likewise the centre of *his* world.

There we have, in that little word "I", the *whole problem of life*, the potential answer to all the questions that make life so grievous to be borne—from the petty daily bickerings of husband and wife or father and child to the so-called social and political problems, and the whole question of war and peace— all is implicit in the fact that each "I" is the central concern in its own existence, the axis on which everything—really everything—turns. And because there are so many of these centres and each considers as a matter of course that it is the hub of the universe, there is no peace, but universal strife. Hence war, greedy exploitation, the struggle for existence, and all the pain and distress which flow from those things. All is rooted in the fact that the ego cannot help regarding itself as the axis on which the world revolves.

Now, realizing to some extent that this is the case, and that life cannot be run on these lines, men seek to adjust their conflicting claims by mutual agreement, and to reach compromises, by which each gets his due. This is described as justice. Just as two neighbours, each of whom lays claim to a right of way, a bit of land, strike a bargain, meet each other half way and say: I will renounce part of my claim, you will renounce part of yours and then we shall settle the matter. But this kind of solution is difficult to achieve and uncertain in result—for the most part it is apt to break down and if it does work, then both parties are inclined to feel that they have not received their full rights. This is what happens among neighbours and likewise among nations. By this means the problem of the claimful self is only barely and only apparently solved.

And now we hear *in the Bible too* this same note "I" struck, but its tone is quite other than that emitted by the sound of the human "I". It has the numinous resonance of the divine. "I am the Lord, thy God." At once we note this: every human-sounding "I" must be silent before that reverberation. Whether there is a higher or a lower, a mightier or a weaker party is a matter of utter indifference in face of that divine I-sound, and for the very reason that the claim of each individual to be the centre of his own world is at once called in question by the mere fact that He, the Lord, who says, "I am the Lord, thy God", implies in exactly the same way to every claimful human being: You are wrong, you are by no means the centre of your world, and the master of your life, it is *I who am the centre* of the world and the Lord of your life, indeed of every life, whether it be great or small, pious or impious, Christian or heathen. What-ever you may say is unimportant, for the important thing is what I say, I the Lord, thy God. And whereas, among we men, if someone comes along and says: "You look out, I am going to do this or that", we immediately stand up for ourselves and prepare to do battle, the situation is very different when this divine I addresses us. The truth is then borne in on us: We con-fess that we are not the centre of the world and have not the right to dictate the why and wherefore, He alone has that right and that place. For He is the Creator, the Lord of all worlds, the almighty, eternal and holy God. Then we must bow our heads and prostrate ourselves in silence and adoration: "God is here, let all be silent within us, and bow before Him." Then we recognize that He, not ourselves, is the ultimate Arbitrator, and that we have not the last word. He, not we, knows how every-thing is as it is and how everything should be. We have only an insignificant I which He allocates to its proper place, whereas He is the Almighty to whom alone honour belongs. Thus in the Old Testament the prophets address us, summoning men in the name of God: "Thus saith the Lord: I am the Lord, thy God...."

Now the fact of central importance in the New Testament is

just this, viz. that this "I am" is spoken not out of the mouth of God, but out of the mouth of *a man* who declares without qualification: "I am.... I am the way, the truth, and the life." Is not the man crazy who so speaks, so that it would be better to shut him up in the lunatic asylum than to pay any attention to him? Such was the feeling of the Scribes and Pharisees: "He is a blasphemer and has a devil." Yes, indeed; thus to come forward with these claims, such as only God makes through the mouth of His prophets, is utterly fantastic. And to say in fact: "I am the way, the truth, and the life"—is it not madness for a man to speak so?

That is the decisive issue in the New Testament; not the question whether Jesus may legitimately make these claims, but the question whether we are willing to recognize them. For long, theologians have thought they could evade this issue by pointing out that Jesus speaks thus only in the Gospel of John, not, however, in the synoptic gospels. John made of the historical Jesus a god, which is what He neither was nor claimed to be. We must hold fast to the primitive tradition concerning Jesus as we find it in the first three Gospels. But this thesis was short-lived. To-day every exponent of the New Testament knows that in the first three as in the fourth Gospel, we hear the voice of that Jesus who utters the "I am" with absolute divine authority, although in the Synoptics the note is more reserved and restrained. The first three evangelists tried to reproduce with the utmost possible accuracy the language of Jesus as He spoke before His resurrection: but the Johannine gospel expresses the truth in the light of the Resurrection, hence much more directly and plainly. He who says: "I am the way, the truth, and the life" is also the One who says: "I am the resurrection and the life." The difference between the two statements lies not in the content, but in the mode of expression. But essentially the same note is struck in the Gospel of St. Matthew where we find: "Ye have heard that it was said to them of old time . . . but I say unto you"; or in speaking of Himself as Son of Man: "The Son of Man came not to be ministered unto but to minister and to give His life a ransom for many." No; if you read the first three Gospels attentively, you hear in them the echoes of that voice which declares in the Gospel of John: "I am the way, the truth, and the life."

What now is the implication, if a man may legitimately speak so? In the Old Testament prophets, the phrase always was, very modest yet wonderfully majestic: "Thus saith the Lord." Then all Israel knew that this man was uttering the words which God had placed in his mouth, that he was only a messenger of God, the bearer of a divine epistle, as it were. His personality was effaced behind the word, the message. In the New Testament, with Jesus, the emphasis is quite different. There we read: "Come unto Me all ye that are weary and heavy-laden, and *I* will refresh you." There the reply to the question: "Art thou He?" is "Yea, I am He." "Who art thou?" He who may legitimately say "I", as only God can do. In His living Person, He embodies what with the prophets is only the word inspired by God. The prophet says, "The *word* of the Lord came unto me", but Jesus says: "*I* have come." That means—He is the Messiah promised by the prophets, the Christ, and thus He through whom God inaugurates His kingdom on earth, He in whom God Himself is present to redeem mankind. "God was in Christ reconciling the world unto Himself."

Now what *difference* does this make to us, to our ego of which we spoke at the beginning? What difference does it make whether a prophet says: "Thus saith the Lord"—"I am the Lord thy God" or whether now a man, Jesus, lives on earth and can rightly say: "I am the way, the truth, and the life"? Let me anticipate. Many people believe, of course, that Jesus is the Son of God; they have no hesitation in confessing: "I believe in the divinity of Jesus Christ, in redemption through His blood, in His resurrection and ascension—in short, I believe everything which the orthodox catechism contains." Do you suppose, my friends, that this is pleasing to God and that He replies: "Those are just the right sort of people, the orthodox in whom I am well pleased?" Do you really think so? Cast your thoughts back to what I said at the beginning about the "I" which is the inevitable axis of our lives. Does this so-called right belief affect in the slightest degree that situation? The mere fact that I acknowledge God to be my sovereign Lord, Jesus Christ to be my Redeemer, has made not the slightest difference to my self-preoccupation, to the ever-recurrent "I". And yet that is the main point. If the self-centred personality is not revolutionized, then the whole structure of Christian orthodoxy is useless.

But now let us consider our text rightly. It says first, "*I am the way*", and concludes: "No man cometh to the Father but by me." Hence the point at issue is a way by which we must come to the Father. Merely to believe in God and to know about God is not what counts with Jesus. What matters is that we should take a certain path—a path that leads to the Father. Jesus does not aim at giving us the true orthodox beliefs, but at leading us into communion with the Father. This communion with the Father, life anchored in the eternity of God, is only possible through the mediation of Jesus. How so? Jesus is the living Way; one must accompany Him on that road, and not stop short at believing in Him. But the way of Jesus is the way of the cross. Again the point is not that we are able to say: I believe in redemption wrought by His blood. Jesus attaches no importance to our thus reciting an article of the creed. The point is rather that we should accompany Jesus on the way to the cross, and then and then alone do we come to the Father.

And now we begin to understand what all this has to do with our perpetual "I; I". When indeed we accompany Jesus on the way to the cross, then the "I" is finally disposed of, silenced, slain. For the way of the cross is symbolized by the strait gate, the tiny door, which we cannot pass through unless we stoop. The proud ego which carries its head so high must bend, even to the earth, in order to pass through the strait gate—such is the way to the Father. The apostle Paul especially has explained in his letters what it means to die with Christ, to accept His Cross as at one and the same time God's judgment upon us and the instrument whereby He reconciles us to Himself. By this communion in the way of Jesus Christ the Crucified it happens that at last the panting breath of the restless ego expires and that it can now no longer cry out with its assertive "I", "I". The "I" which usurps centrality is destroyed, there is an end to all such thoughts as "If only other people were as I am", "I am certainly in the right, it is other people who are wrong"; there is an end to this whole reign and self-glorification of the human ego. At the cross, it happens that the old man can only exclaim: "God be merciful to me a sinner", and "I thank you, O God, that you go on loving me in spite of myself."

In all this is implied the understanding of the second phrase: "*I am the truth.*" We suppose—and this is all part of our self-centredness—that it is we who know what is true and can make an appraisement of all things. But again it comes about through Jesus Christ that we are healed of this blindness which imagines the truth to be in ourselves, and that we now seek it no longer in ourselves but in Him. He must tell us of course how things stand with us. He must tell us that we abide not in the light of truth but in the darkness of falsehood and perversity. He must tell us how we can gain deliverance from this falsehood and find the truth, namely, by recognizing through Him that truth resides in God, in His sovereignty and not in the false sovereignty of our own selves. But again we can only come to grasp this as we see in Jesus Christ the love of God seeking us and bestowing itself upon us. Again and again we refuse to believe —and often orthodox Christians believe it least of all—that our claimful ego is the abode of all falsehood, negation and crookedness, and that only in the revealed love of God do we see the truth and meaning of life. Until we come to the full apprehension and realization of this, it must be that we do not simply "believe in Jesus" in a facile and superficial manner, but that we come unto Him as to a fire which burns away our dross. Our "I" must die in Him so that we learn to know the truth which is nothing other than love, and this knowledge is then no longer a merely objective knowledge which does not radically affect us, nor sway our personal lives, but a knowledge which is through and through subjective, changing the whole direction of our ego.

Now we are in a position to understand also the third phrase: "*I am the life.*" We suppose, especially so long as we are healthy and capable of energetically accomplishing our purposes, that we have life in ourselves. Life is then nothing other than the power of our "I, I", exploiting its intrinsic resources. But this kind of life, Jesus reveals to us, is not life at all, but death both for ourselves and for others. We bring death to ourselves and to those around us. We ourselves suffer from our insatiable ego and make other people suffer from it. In communion with Jesus, however, this ego is transformed so that instead of its ever-recurrent "I" it learns to say "Thou". And in that lies the beginning of new life. As death is of the essence of that old egoistic life, so real life, life in the love of God, eternal life which knows no death, is integral to this new life, lived in the "Thou".

The mystery of Jesus lies in the fact that behind His cross stands His resurrection. We cannot ever pierce that mystery. But it is a mighty indissoluble fact and on that fact rests the life of the Christian Church. Without the resurrection of Jesus Christ from the dead the disciples would have fled into the night of time and Jesus would have been forgotten. The fact that they saw again the Crucified as the Risen One and learned to apprehend His ever-living Presence—that and that alone inspired in them the certainty: He it is in whom God dwelt among us and dwells among us now for evermore. It was this inner assurance, this experience of the living presence and power of Jesus Christ, which raised in them a new life out of the death of their old Adam—life with Christ, life in the love of God, life of which they knew: death cannot destroy this life, for it flows from the eternal life of God. Nothing can separate us from the love of God, not even death.

Hence this word is true—"I am the way, the truth, and the life: no man cometh to the Father but by me." In this threefold "I", Jesus exposes our falsehood and confronts us with the truth: He opposes His eternal life to the death in which we are implicated. He does so by showing us the way which leads to the Father.

Just think, my friends, we must travel a road in order to reach a goal. A road with which you are not personally acquainted remains a mere line on the map. It avails nothing to know all sorts of things about Jesus, to know the entire catechism by heart. That in itself is useless; you must *travel* along this way. In the New Testament, this travelling is called faith: to accompany Jesus on the way to the cross, to the point where our old ego is burnt up and out of the fires of transformation there springs to birth a new man who no longer says "I", but lives in the love of God, in the "Thou" of Christ. Such is the life of faith—this transmutation of the "I" into the "Thou" of God. Of that faith, the New Testament declares: "Whosoever believeth on me, *hath* eternal life."

SERVICE

Let a man so account of us, as of ministers of Christ, and stewards of the mysteries of God. Here, moreover, it is required in stewards, that a man be found faithful.

1 Cor. 4: 1–2

When ye shall have done all the things that are commanded you, say, We are unprofitable servants; we have done that which it was our duty to do.

Luke 17: 10

TO-DAY is, as you know, the last time that I shall have the privilege of preaching the Word of God to you here in this dear Fraumünster before I leave for the Far East. Hence I would like to talk to you about that which binds into a coherent whole these two phases of my ministry—that which I have fulfilled in the past and that which still lies in the future. For it is one and the same consideration which has inspired me, both whenever I have prepared to preach in this cathedral and when I decided to accept a call to work in that far-off and strange world of the East. It was 41 years ago when we theological students were ordained here in this cathedral by Professor von Schulthess-Rechberg, who was acting in the name of our Church convocation, and when we received from the Church of Zürich that first stage of ordination described by the beautiful title: *Verbi Divini Minister*, servant of the divine Word. Of all the many titles which I have received in the course of these 41 years, this one is by far the loveliest and the most important. It is the very description which the apostle Paul used to describe his own calling and of which he speaks in our text. Perhaps on this special occasion I may be allowed to say that every time, before climbing these pulpit steps, I have tried to realize afresh what an extraordinary privilege it is to be allowed to preach the gospel of Jesus Christ to a great congregation. I have never felt worthy to do so but have ever deemed it a special and un-deserved grace of God that He should have deigned to allow me, all unworthy, to accomplish this greatest task which any man can: to preach about the splendour of our heavenly and eternal destiny in His name and by His command. The title *Verbi Divini Minister* has often almost crushed me and yet, ever anew, made me supremely happy.

It is in fact something quite amazing that a man should come before other men whom he does not know and tell them: I am speaking to you in the name and by the command of the All-highest, the Creator of heaven and earth, the Judge in whose presence we must all one day stand and give account of our-selves; in the name of the Redeemer God who in Jesus Christ has disclosed to us the secret of His will and plan of universal salvation. Such a man must not produce the fruits of his own wisdom, were it never so brilliant and well thought-out, but is called to expound the Word of God alone. Can a man legiti-mately claim to voice the Word of God? Does not such a claim imply monstrous presumption, indeed madness? One might perhaps believe it to be possible in the case of the apostle Paul, the chosen servant of God, or in the case of a prophet—but how can one believe it of an ordinary man who is no better than others, not even cleverer than thousands of others and who can-not say with the prophets—God has placed His words in my mouth, as the prophets Isaiah, Jeremiah and Ezekiel, for exam-ple, repeatedly declare?

How then can one of us stand forth before his fellow-men with such an unheard-of pretension and say: "*Let a man so account of me as a minister of Christ and steward of the mysteries of God*"? Does the mere fact of passing a theological examination and being ordained by the authority of the assembled Church make one a minister of Christ and a steward of the mysteries of God? Certainly not. For both these qualifications spring from human arrangements, and how could men declare one com-petent to fulfil what lies in the sole power and authority of God? But now, just think—the mystery of the Body of Christ, not of the institutional Church, but of the communion of Jesus, resides in the fact that the fundamental substance of the revelation is made known to every member of the Body and elucidated by the Holy Spirit. The mysteries of the divine will are entrusted not to the priest as such, nor to the professor of theology as such, but to the Christian as a Christian, and for this reason every mature Christian should in principle be a preacher of the Word, in so far as he has known and experienced the reality of Jesus Christ as Saviour. Theological study helps only in so far as it gives one greater familiarity with Holy Scripture and greater facility in exposition of revealed truth. But in essence the words of this text—minister of Christ and steward of the divine mysteries—apply to every single Christian. By the word of the apostles and the age-long ministry of the Church we have received these treasures and are called to distribute what we have received. This is our great prerogative—that we Christians are initiated into the mysteries of salvation; that we know the purpose which God has towards us and to what end He is guiding us. You—members of the Christian congregation—have the inestimable advantage of knowing this: that God is love, that God bestows Himself and His eternal life upon us in Jesus Christ. This is not the privilege of priest and theologian, but the privilege of all Christians as such. You are all, even though you are not ordained, ministers of Christ and stewards of the mysteries of God. The task of the preacher is simply again and again to remind the congregation of Christ's flock of what it already knows, and to confirm it in the possession of what it already has.

Now of course there are thousands who do not yet know the truth, who are not yet members of the Body of Christ and the Christian congregation. And the function of the apostle, as of those who with him are commissioned by the Church and sent forth to distribute what they have received, lies in the first instance with these unbelievers. This ministry we usually describe as *missionary* work, though the description as a rule savours of something very specialized, departmental and fervently pious. Missionaries, we think, these are men trained by a missionary society and then sent forth to heathen lands to bring the benighted heathen within reach of the Gospel message. My friends, that represents far too limited a view of missionary endeavour. In the primitive Christian community, every Christian was a missionary. The Gospel of Jesus Christ expanded throughout Europe not, in the first instance, by the agency of specialist missionaries, but because every Christian felt himself obliged and called to give out to others who had it not, the truth which he himself had received and which was to him the most precious thing in the world. And among us moderns, it must come to that again. It is your duty as Christians to impart to others what you have received and what you very well know is the best that you have.

And hence what I am now preparing to do is nothing at all special, but something which belongs to the essence of the Christian vocation as such. It is simply not right and not in accordance with the will of Christ that we reserve to ourselves the treasures of His gospel, as if the latter were a European affair, a religion for the white race. I do not think that God has any peculiar fondness for the white man or the European. He is the Creator of all mankind and He wills that all should know Him as He has revealed Himself in Jesus Christ—who was an Asiatic. How could He not wish that the thousands of millions of Asiatics should come to know Him?

God's mysteries are committed to the stewardship of the Christian apostle. Asiatics too have their religion and some Asiatic peoples, as, for example, Indians, have to some extent imposing systems of religion. Hence we hear it said: "Why need we press our religion upon them who do not desire it?" Is this not in fact an expression of diehard European imperialism? Whoever speaks thus has not yet understood very deeply the Gospel of Jesus Christ. For the latter is not one religion among many. It is, properly speaking, not a religion at all, but the manifestation of the life and power and reality of God. What the other so-called religions have is no doubt a certain glimmer of the divine light, but not that light itself. We do not know why God has so willed it, but it is definitively the case that He has revealed the mystery of His love only in Jesus Christ, His Son. Only in Him has He revealed Himself as the God who loves sinful man, who forgives our sins, and has destined us to the consummation of eternal life in His Kingdom. Those other religions know nothing of this goal, and of that love of God which is turned towards sinful man. *There* lies the divine mystery which God has revealed in Jesus Christ and in no other. Hence the word of the apostle is true, that in no other is salvation, nor is there any other name whereby we can be saved (Acts 4: 12).

For this reason we owe it to other peoples to make known unto them these mysteries. Certainly there are multitudes at home who do not know the truth of the Gospel, and there is, therefore, work enough to be done here. But the same situation existed in the time of the apostles. Truly Paul would have had enough to do in Jerusalem and in Palestine. Yet God bade him carry the Gospel to those peoples who knew least about Him. Indeed, it was precisely to the most remote and neglected that Paul felt a special obligation. After evangelizing the Near East, the region of modern Turkey, and then taking the Gospel to Greece and finally reaching Rome, the apostle wished to go still further afield, to Spain, which to his ideas represented the limits of the West.

And so it is with me. As a steward of the divine mysteries, it is not for me myself to determine in what directions they are to be dispensed. One must hold oneself at the disposal of God to go where He wills. And the fact now is that the call has come to me from Japan and I am convinced that it is not merely a call of man, but of God. I am ready to obey it.

In thinking over these things—and that I had to do, of course, since we can deceive ourselves even about a sense of divine mission—it became clear to me why God wished me to go there. For Japan is a country which is destined to be of great significance both for the future of Asia and the future of humanity. In contradistinction to India and China, the Japanese people enjoy universal education. Whereas in India only eight out of a hundred people can read (and in China it is no better but rather worse), in Japan there are no illiterates. Further, Japan is a country equipped with the amenities of modern civilization, especially with industrial technology, and thus is prepared at once to assume a commanding position among the peoples of Asia.

On the other hand, its intellectual and spiritual foundations are rent, perhaps one may say undermined. It is experiencing a religious and spiritual vacuum, as is perhaps no other nation on the earth, and that stands in a curious and dangerous contrast to its high level of general culture. In short, Japan is, from the point of view of missionary strategy, the country which must form the focus of our attention. I do not dare to go so far as to say that Japan specially needs the Gospel, nor that Japan is specially prepared to receive the Gospel. But I do boldly affirm that, from the standpoint of the Christian mission, Japan is a country deserving of quite special attention. Now there is not indeed any lack of missionaries in this country, but there are lacking preachers of the Gospel who in some degree are capable of handling the problems with which modern education and modern science confronts any exponent of Christian doctrine. In this respect I am in some measure specially equipped as a result of my previous experience of life.

But I would not spontaneously have conceived the plan of devoting the last years of my intellectual maturity to the Japanese people. The fact is that the impulse to do so, the outward call, came from Japan itself. I can only say that in the circumstances I believe I recognize in the invitation of the International Christian University of Tokyo a real call of God, and, since my wife shares my opinion, I have been so bold as to accept this call. What will come of it lies in the hands of God. I do not myself know, I am not setting out with any specially keen expectations, it is only that I do not want to be disobedient to what I believe is the divine will. Nor do I think I would be justified in counting on any special praise or recognition for my action and decision. For this reason I have taken as my text to-day, along with the word of the apostle Paul, that of the Lord Jesus Himself which describes the life work of a servant of Jesus in very sober, not to say severe, terms: "*When you have done all the things that are commanded you, say, We are unprofitable servants; we have done that which it was our duty to do.*"

My friends, I do not dare to hope that I shall ever arrive at the stage of being able to say: "I have done all that was commanded me" or, in the Pauline phrase, "as a servant or steward, have been found faithful." On the contrary, I have never felt like saying that up to now, but rather have felt that I have fallen far, far, short of my duty. In the course of my life I have received much recognition, far too much in comparison with others. Much love and human respect and regard have been showered upon me, so that in this as in many other things I am constrained to say: I have been pampered and spoilt, I have really no reason to complain. And if, in this regard, things should not go so well with me in Japan as has hitherto been the case, I should still not have the least right to complain and am firmly resolved never to do so. I know that I have no claim upon God.

And yet I cannot fail to ask Him that He would be pleased to give me success, not for my sake personally, but for the sake of His will and His honour. The Japanese people sorely need the Gospel. The nations of the world deeply need to come to know Jesus Christ, the love of God and life in the fullness of divine love. That is the divine mystery to the service of which I am committed, and to serve which with all my powers is my firm determination. Hence, because this service is the will of God, I would like to ask you to support us by your prayers. For intercession too is the service of Christ and is not merely desired of you but commanded from on high, and in regard to that service the word about the steward and servant is equally applicable. So let us then remain steadfast and unmovable in that common service, and so abide in fellowship with each other for time and eternity.